Strength
From Above

Forming the Basis for a Fulfilling Life

FEB
2020

BRYAN

Strength
From Above
Forming the Basis for a Fulfilling Life

MAY GOD CONTINUE TO GIVE YOU THE STRENGTH YOU NEED FOR THE JOURNEY. BLESS YOU, MY BROTHER

Douglas J. Glada

Strength From Above
by Douglas J. Glada

Published by

First Page Solutions

Kelowna BC Canada

ISBN 10: 1-988226-19-8
ISBN 13: 978-1-988226-19-4

CONTENTS

Foreword

I have known Doug for almost 35 years, as fellow-elder and pastor, salesman, and friend. Some write books for publicity; others write books simply to be heard. Doug has waited years to put into writing a message that has emerged out of his personal revelation of God and his daily journey with God. His spiritual legacy is seasoned with wisdom that has been garnered through overcoming many tests to faith. When I think of Doug, I think of faithfulness: faithfulness to God and His Word, to His Church, to his leaders, to his wife, Sue and family, and to his friends. He has now faithfully committed this book to the Holy Spirit to pass it forward: what has brought him strength from God will also bring you strength.

- David Kalamen - Founding Pastor/CEO, Kelowna Christian Center Society

Introduction

This book has been birthed out of my deep desire to share the Word of God in a simple but profound way. I am convinced God's Word is so powerful that one little word from Him can change a life forever, and so, I have set out to write these short chapters in a conversational and devotional style which is aimed at the reader's heart. My prayer is that these words would inspire you to continue your own intimate journey with the Lord. Let Him speak to you through His Word, let Him guide you by His Spirit, and let Him bring you into new opportunities and adventures which are awaiting you in Christ.

Section One

Surrender

" *The action of yielding one's person or giving up the possession of something especially into the power of another.*

Merriam-Webster

Strength from Heaven

Luke 22:42, 43 – Saying, Father, if you be willing, remove this cup from me: nevertheless, not my will, but yours, be done. And there appeared an angel unto him from heaven, strengthening him.

On the night of his betrayal, in the garden of Gethsemane, we catch a rare glimpse of Jesus, facing what appears to have been, the most difficult hour of his life. We have never seen him in this state before. He is down on his knees and struggling under the crushing weight and realization of what is ahead. I am sure that Jesus was not struggling over the terrible torture and pain of the scourging and crucifixion, as horrific as that would be, as much as He was struggling over the appalling thought of bearing the sin of the world and thus driving himself away from his Father.

He had enjoyed a very intimate and

unbroken relationship with his Father God every day of his life, and now, at this darkest of hours, it is the Father that He calls out to. 'Father, if you are willing.' Jesus appeals to the tenderness of his Father and, for a split second of time, asked for this ordeal to pass. He knew that there was no other way but, Jesus the man, in this heavy, crushing moment, identified with all men, he identified with the tendency to take another route to the throne, to sidestep the cross, and to avoid the intense hardships and sufferings of life.

This nightmare of a test is described by Jesus as a cup that He must drink. All of His life the only cup He knew was the cup of joy and fellowship with God, the cup that runs over with blessing and goodness. Now he must drink a different cup, a cup of the darkest and most hideous thing known to mankind; the cup of that poison that separated Adam from the sweetest of friendships; the cup that has infected all mankind; the cup of sin.

An eternity seems to hang in the balance as

Jesus reels beneath the burden of the plan of God. Angels are, no doubt, hushed as they wait and watch in anticipation. We can imagine them saying, What will this man do? How will he choose? Thousands of years ago, in another garden, a man chose his own way over God's way and thus broke the heart of the Father God and started a destructive chain reaction of sin and death. How would this Last Adam choose? It seems that He is asking for exemption from the will of God, he is asking for special treatment. Oh no! This can't be. Wait. Hold on, the angels say, He is about to speak again. Nevertheless. What did He say? Nevertheless. Hallelujah! He said nevertheless!

Oh! How thankful we should be for that one word; nevertheless. All of eternity hinged on that history-making word. Even though I am under intense pressure to give in, and even though I have done nothing wrong or deserving of death, Father, nevertheless, not my will, not my choice or my determination, but what you determine, Father. Your will, your choice, what you determine is the best way and the only way. George Mueller once wrote, 'When we forsake the ways of the Lord during the hour of trial, the food for faith will be lost.' Jesus chose God's way, and thus his faith was nourished, and He was divinely strengthened to press onward and to boldly face the Cross.

Thank God for Jesus! What an example to all of us who struggle in our own 'Gethsemane,' wanting our own way, attempting to avoid the inevitable challenges and hardships of life. I believe that we can also pray that prayer along with Jesus, 'Not my will, Father, but your will be done.' As we bend our will to His will, Heaven's strength will come flowing in and we can arise and journey into the day and into our destiny.

Fall on the Rock and be Broken

Luke 20:18 – Whoever shall fall upon that stone shall be broken, but on whomever it shall fall, it will grind him to powder.

The stone is unchangeable. The stone or, the rock, to the Jewish culture, represents God; steady, faithful, ancient, time-tested, always the same, secure, powerful and weighty. The Psalmist said, 'He is my Rock.' He is my Touchstone. The rock is always the same and is no respecter of persons or circumstance. The rock represents the laws or principles of God. In Stephen Covey's terms, the rock is the unmovable lighthouse versus the approaching large vessel. We can choose to willingly surrender and fall upon the rock, lay our lives on it, and yield to its strength and un-changeableness, or, we can suffer the consequences. We have this choice now, but it seems that it will be removed one day; we will no longer have a choice.

If we fall on the rock, we will be broken. When something is broken, we usually see it as needing to be fixed, but in God's economy, broken is a good thing. There are things in our life that need to be broken – our stubbornness, our selfishness, our sinfulness, our maliciousness, and many other things such as; hatred, strife, ego, pride, envy, gossip etcetera; these things need to be broken. But our text does not say that sinful things need to be broken, it goes much deeper than that, it says that 'whoever' falls upon the rock shall be broken. We are to be broken. The self needs to be broken. The fallen identity, the humanly invented meaning of our existence needs to be broken, likewise, so should false belief systems and flawed motives.

I must choose to daily fall on the rock or one day it – God laws, His principles, His un-changeableness, His authority, the weight and the force of who He is will fall on me. The load and weightiness of that rock will crush the life out of me; it will grind me to powder. So, the question is, Will I be broken by choice, or ground to powder by force?

To fall on the rock is to willingly let go and let God, to stop striving and release yourself, your life, and your security, take it all and place it on the Eternal Rock; the only genuinely secure thing there is.

God's Laws of Process and Growth

John 12:24 - Verily, verily, I say unto you, Except a grain of wheat fall into the ground and die, it abides alone: but if it die, it brings forth much fruit.

Jesus speaks to us of a seed and its process; it must fall into the ground and die. Both of those ideas are rejected by our positive-thinking, you-can-do-it culture. Firstly, we do not want to fall and, secondly, we certainly do not want to die, but Jesus says it is essential that both happen. The seed will remain an isolated and solitary seed if it does not surrender to this seemingly contradictory route. The seed must leave one environment and enter another environment for it to change and grow. Do we wish to continue to cling to what we know? Are we going to hang on to the comfort of familiarity? You have probably heard people say, 'I'd rather stick with the devil I know than the devil I don't know', meaning, that even though circumstances may be hard and undesirable, many times we are afraid to step out into something that we do not know so, we stay with the undesirable thing that we do know. Sadly though, we will never know the possibilities of what could be if we remain in the same known place, abiding as a seed. There was an Abraham within Abram, but he would never have developed into the father of a multitude had he not left the familiar status quo behind. Elisha left his parents and his oxen, David left the sheepfold, Peter and John left their nets, Saul of Tarsus left the Pharisees, and all of God's men and women must leave in order for the promise of Jesus to be fulfilled; 'he shall receive an hundredfold.'

The seed represents astounding potential. The DNA of a full-grown oak tree is in the acorn, but there are laws of process that need to be observed, submitted to and obeyed. It is the will of God for that seed to grow and to become all that lies dormant within it, but there are laws of God that determine the unfolding of his will. If that seed never falls into the soil, thus surrendering itself to the death procedure, the capabilities and possibilities of the seed will never be released. The fall, the yielding, the surrendering of the seed must take place first; we must say with Jesus, 'not my will but thine be done.' The seed, by remaining a seed, controls what it will always be; however, we need to release control if we are to become what God wants us to be.

The seed must enter the ground, into the unseen territory and into a new environment. God works through environment; nothing develops on its own. Neither the seed nor the man will ever grow without being placed around the right people and within the right setting. Once the seed has fallen into the soil, it must begin to die. Oh! How we recoil from that word and from the idea of death, but when we understand that death simply means a separation, then we gain a new appreciation for the method that God has chosen. It will be necessary for the seed to be stripped of its protective shell for the nutrients of the soil to penetrate and do their mysterious work. We will never reach the levels of development that are written into our DNA until we remove our self-defence systems and become open and vulnerable.

If we do not submit to this God-ordained way, Jesus informs us that we will abide alone, which is another way of saying that we will remain a single, solitary seed; lots of potential but sadly, no change and no results. However, if we do yield and surrender entirely, placing ourselves in the soil of God's choosing, we can expect a life of consistent growth, undeniable influence, multiplied productivity and deeply satisfying fulfillment. Let go of your life and enter by faith into the unseen life of unending possibilities with God.

God's Idea of Greatness

Matthew 18:4 – Whoever therefore shall humble himself as this little child, the same is greatest in the kingdom of Heaven.

God's idea of greatness and the process for obtaining it are vastly different from this world's idea. Firstly, it is important to realize that He is not against greatness. They asked Him, 'Who is the greatest?' If greatness were wrong, He would have immediately corrected them. He might have said something like this, 'Now boys, you should know better, everyone is equal in the kingdom of God, no one is greater than another.' However, He did not correct them. He did not brush off the idea of greatness. The kingdom of Heaven is not a uniform, bland and mindless community, but it is a progressive, enthusiastic, forward moving and productive society. Please do not misunderstand me; we are all precious to God and equal in value, but we are not and never shall be, equal in roles, function, or capabilities. We all have amazing potential, but those who are the greatest are those who take the initiative, use what they have been given and develop.

This verse is teaching us that even though the idea of greatness is not wrong, quite often our definition of greatness and our motives for greatness are wrong. The prophet Jeremiah once asked the question, 'Are you seeking great things for yourself? Seek them not.' Jesus said that humility is the pathway to greatness. So, instead of focusing on being great and our status in life, we should focus on humility and give that a priority in our lives.

Humility is one of those qualities that we do not hear much about, even though it is essential for building a solid foundation for life. What is humility? Among other things it is surrendering to the will of God and His plan no matter what process it takes you through. Joseph's life is a good example of that. His humility and the will of God took him from the deep pit to the harsh prison to the luxurious palace. Joseph surrendered to difficulties and accepted subservient tasks, but he also must have had the humility to accept the huge responsibility of promotion when it finally came. Someone has said that our greatest fear may not be failure but success, because with success comes larger responsibilities. With failure comes sympathy and the rationalization that says, 'Oh well, I tried.' When God spoke to Moses about going in front of Pharaoh to demand the release of the Israelites, Moses resisted out of some form of what we might call humility, but God was less than impressed. Moses had to surrender and accept with humility the high place of responsibility that God had asked him to take.

Childishness is a trait that holds us back from growth and it desperately needs to be removed from our lives, but childlikeness is a quality that we must retain for the rest of our lives; indeed, it is the key to the kingdom of Heaven. Little children have much to teach us, they are open to new ideas and suggestions; they do not say, 'I know that already.' Children are teachable which means that they are without pride. If humility is the path to greatness, then pride must be the path to diminishment and destruction. Pride is the great hindrance to our advancement in God's plan and purpose. Pride is resisted by God, humility is reinforced. Pride says, 'I cannot,' but humility says, 'I can.' Pride says, 'I will not,' humility says, 'I will.'

Jesus, by using a child as an example, elevated the status of all children for all time. The world does not value children, in fact, it gives children a clear message; 'You are not valuable or important until you grow up to be something.' This is the opposite of the way Jesus views the young ones. He sees them as complete and perfect and far beyond any price that could be calculated. He, Himself, was and still is the ultimate Child of His heavenly Father, and the highest example of greatness.

Follow Him

Matthew 16:24 – Then said Jesus to His disciples, If any man will come after me, let him deny himself and take up his cross and follow me.

Jesus had just spoken to His disciples about the Cross, foretelling them that He would be killed and rise again the third day. Peter, in fine form, took Jesus aside and rebuked Him because he was convinced that suffering could never be the will of God. Jesus spoke some of His strongest words as He corrected Peter and set him straight. He then issued some tough words to the rest of us.

If any man will come after me. This phrase answers a lot for me. Is Jesus ahead of me in the direction of my life? If I look at where I am headed, do I see the Lord in front of me? He is Lord. He is in charge. He is supposed to be in front, I am to come after Him. He must always be first I am always to be after. One day all the universe will clearly see Him for who He is; indeed, every knee shall bow. Wise people practice that now.

If any man will. Anyone can choose to come and to follow Him. It is a decision. It is a choice. It is a God-given freedom, and it is mine alone to make. I can choose to put Him first. It is not dictated by my life and circumstances. I cannot blame my situation, my work, my family or any other thing. No! Whatever place I am in right now, good or bad, I have the choice to put Him first. Where there is a will, there is a way.

Let him deny himself. To deny is to choose to abstain. I might be denying myself that piece of pie, or denying a purchase, or denying myself the free time that I had set aside for my interests. It can be very hard to deny certain things, but Jesus never said to deny things; He said, deny yourself. My self-life must be denied. I must disown and disavow my self-centred life. Do not misunderstand me. We must take care of ourselves and live a balanced life, but selfishness is never okay. Self-care is good; self-focus is not.

Take up his cross. There is a popular song that is sung in many churches today, and one phrase of it says gratefully to the Lord, 'That You would bear my cross.' It is a beautiful song, and I enjoy the artist, but that phrase contradicts what Jesus said here. We are to take up our cross. There is a Cross that we could never take up, and that is the Cross of Christ. He is the only one who could do that, but there is a personal cross-bearing that must happen in the life of the believer. Now we mustn't get confused about what it means to take up our cross, because there are many non-scriptural ideas about it. The context would indicate that the cross-bearing we are to experience has to do with putting Him first and self-denial. Luke's account says we are to do this daily, strongly suggesting that this is a big part of our Christian life.

Follow me. The good news about all of this is that Jesus is with us; He is right here. He has, by virtue of His Cross, experienced every imaginable hardship and test and come out of it victoriously. He knows. He understands our humanity. He has already provided for every possible contingency. There is nothing coming in our lives that He has not already foreseen and prepared an answer for. Nothing takes Him by surprise. He is for us, He is with us and He is in us. Our part is simply to follow Him.

Reach for the Sky

1 Timothy 2:8 - I will therefore that men pray everywhere, lifting up holy hands, without wrath and doubting.

Paul specifically exhorts the men to pray. A close look at the average prayer meeting tells us that a lot of the women are already praying. It does seem that it is more natural for women to pray but for men, we want to fix things, or simply work harder, or get a job done with our hands.

This verse tells us that men should pray and lift up holy hands. We are told to take those hands, which represent our ability and strength and lift them up in prayer. To lift them up is the opposite of putting them to work. Lift them up in surrender, yielding them to the Lord. Don't use your hands, let God use his hand to accomplish. I think, when facing difficulties, our tendency as men is to simply work harder but, when things do not go well, we fall into either wrath or doubting.

Prayer is the antidote to both those tendencies. If we pray, then we can trust that God's hand is working; we don't have to yield to doubt. If we pray, then we can let go of all the ill-will or unforgiveness and anger; we can allow God's love to fill our hearts. Anger might also be our tendency when it comes to certain things not working out the way we thought they would. Maybe we are not where we want to be financially, or in our marriage, or with our job or children. The tendency then might be to become frustrated or angry. We might blame others, ourselves, or even God. We may also give in and begin to doubt the word of God. Are the promises of God true? Why hasn't this or that happened? Maybe at that point we might begin to doubt ourselves. Do we have what it takes? Maybe God can't use me anymore, maybe my wife or children do not need me anymore. No! All these are lies. Prayer brings us into a place of truth, it brings clarity to our thinking and enables us to have God's perspective.

It is also interesting to note that we are told that men should pray everywhere; all men in every locality are to pray. All of us, regardless of our circumstances and status or our geographical location, are to pray. Prayer levels the playing field. No one has more access to the Father than anyone else. We are equal in the place of prayer. Prayer is the answer for all men in all locations. Many times, it feels like we are stuck; stuck in a certain situation or in a certain location but as someone has once said, 'you can get anywhere in the world from where you are right now'. The truth is we do not need to get anywhere but simply to look up and to lift up our hands in prayer. I encourage all men everywhere, before you go out in the morning to use your hands to produce an income and provide for your family, to lift up those holy and sacred hands to your Heavenly Father, the ultimate provider. Let's expect the answers and the solutions that we need right now as we raise our hands and our hearts to the One who is ready, able and willing to use His hands on our behalf. Amen!

Section Two

<u>Faith</u>

" *Complete   trust   or confidence in someone or something.*

Oxford Dictionary

Building the Unseen Life

2 Corinthians 4:18 - While we look not at the things which are seen, but at the things which are not seen: for the things which are seen are temporary; but the things which are not seen are eternal.

This verse describes the daily battle. We live in the world of sense, but we know that this world of sense is not the highest reality. Paul encourages us to 'look' at the things which are not seen. So, there are things which are seen, they are obvious and clearly revealed to the senses. We see them, we hear them, we can touch them, and they exist in a world of time and sense. The five senses are amazing gifts given to us by God to interact with our world. Everything we know comes through those five senses. We saw it, we heard it, and we gained knowledge by using our senses.

But Paul says there is a world outside of time and sense. We are to 'look' at the invisible things. What are those things which are not seen? They are eternal realities. Because we live in this world, it is very easy to walk through this life without realizing or prioritizing the next life. One way to look at things which are not seen is to believe that they exist and to plan accordingly. The life of faith is not based on the things which are seen, or things which are revealed to the senses. The life of faith is based on the things which are not seen, or things which are not revealed to the senses.

There is a striking contrast between things seen and things unseen, things temporary and things eternal. If it is seen, it is temporary. Everything we see is temporary, it is but for a moment or a season, it will not last forever. Everything we do not see is eternal, it will endure through all time, and it will last forever. So, the important question is, what are we looking at? Are we constantly looking at the visible world and directing our lives by it? Or are we constantly looking at the invisible world and basing our decisions on it?

Jesus described two men that built houses by their attitude toward the Word of God. The wise man built his house on a rock-solid foundation by hearing the Word, acting on it and living by it. He 'looked' at things which are not seen. The foolish man built his house on a shifting foundation by ignoring the importance of the Word of God and not having a daily priority of practicing what he heard. Both houses probably looked similar for a time. It wasn't until the storms came that the true nature and strength of the foundation was discovered. The house is the thing which is seen, the foundation is the thing which is not seen. The thing which is seen is subject to the elements and thus to change, the thing which is not seen is hidden below the surface and established upon a rock, so it is unmovable regardless of what comes. Let's walk by faith, focusing on the unseen and continue to build an eternally secure house!

Sleeping by Faith in the Midst of Trouble

Acts 12:6 - And when Herod would have brought him forth, the same night Peter was sleeping between two soldiers, bound with two chains: and the keepers before the door kept the prison.

In this account, we find that Herod had already killed James and had now imprisoned Peter with the intention of doing the same to him. Peter was shackled with chains and kept under close watch by several armed guards. Herod's plan was to bring him out and brutally murder him the next morning. What would we expect that Peter's last night, before his execution, would look like? Would he be writing letters to his loved ones or would he be praying and preparing to meet the Lord face to face? Would he be frantic and worried about all those whom he was about to leave behind? No! We find him sleeping. Was he sleeping because he was so despondent that he had lost all will to survive? Was he sleeping because he was so fatigued from all of his labours for the Lord? I don't think so.

We have the record of another night, several years earlier, when Jesus was in the garden of Gethsemane. That night Jesus had asked Peter to watch and pray with him, but instead Peter was found sleeping. Jesus was not pleased with the fact that Peter could not stay awake and pray for at least one hour. That night in the garden Peter surrendered to the sleep of apathy, the sleep of hopelessness, and the sleep of fear, but the night of his imprisonment Peter slept for a different reason. Peter may have been rebuked for one type of sleep, but he is to be commended for this type, because in this case he was sleeping the sleep of faith. A man that is in an austere prison, bound between two soldiers and awaiting his execution, usually, would be wide awake. But Peter was sleeping so soundly that the angel had to jostle him out of his grogginess.

Why was it that Peter could have such peace at this time? One reason could be something that Jesus had said to Peter just before his ascension, gave him a rock-solid conviction of his future. Jesus had told Peter that when he was old, someone would take him where he did not want to go. 'When he was old.' Peter was told by the Lord that he would indeed be murdered for his faith, but it was to happen when he was old. I can imagine Peter that night in the prison saying to himself, 'I am not old yet, so I cannot die yet. The Lord has a plan to deliver me from this situation. Therefore, I am going to sleep'. Someone has once said that until you have fulfilled the will of God on earth, you are invincible.

This account of Peter reminds me of another story recorded during World War II. London was under a period of intense bombing and almost every night the sirens went off, and people would run to the shelters for safety. One of those that ran to the shelter each night was an older lady, who lived on her own. One night it was noticed that she was missing, and it was assumed that she had been caught in the explosions and was injured or worse. Shortly after she was seen on the street during the day and was asked if everything was alright and that people were concerned about her. She responded by saying that she had been reading in the book of Psalms and came across a verse that stated, 'He that keeps Israel neither slumbers nor sleeps' so she had decided if God was continually awake, then there was no point in both of them losing sleep, so she just went to bed each night and slept soundly through the incessant air raids. Maybe Peter thought the same. Maybe we should think the same. There are different times and seasons and situations in life and not all require the same response. Sometimes we may need to be aggressive in prayer and other times the greatest act of faith may be to simply go to sleep, resting soundly and trusting fully that we are being kept safe by the power of God through faith. God has got you covered, and under the covers is when we sleep best.

Elements of Faith – Part One

Mark 11:22, 23 - And Jesus answered them, Have faith in God. Truly, I say to you, whoever says to this mountain, 'Be taken up and thrown into the sea,' and does not doubt in his heart, but believes that what he says will come to pass, it will be done for him.

I remember years ago, as I read these words early in the morning, in a flash I saw that there were three necessary and connected elements of faith and they corresponded to verse 23, 24 and 25.

There are some things that need to be removed from our life and, it will take this aspect of faith for progress to be made. The mountain represents anything that stands in the way of the plan of God and is not His will for our lives. A mountain is a large and looming obstacle that blocks sight of anything lying beyond it. We are hemmed in by the

mountain and quite often we get used to
seeing it and then surrender to the lie that it
will always be there and that there is nothing
we can do about it. However, in contrast to
this way of thinking, Jesus said that we must
confront the mountain, face it and speak to it
directly. Many times, the mountain on the
inside may be bigger and more of a challenge
than the mountain on the outside. The
mountain on the outside represents a gigantic
problem. It may be a financial debt or huge
need, it may be a sickness or physical
limitation, or it could be opposition to a dream
that God has put in your heart to accomplish.
One thing that we know for sure, the
mountain must be removed and for that to
happen, our attitude has got to change; first
we must deal with the mountain of doubt and
uncertainty that is on the inside of us. We
certainly cannot be mountain-movers if we see
ourselves as helpless victims of the
circumstances of life. We definitely cannot be
mountain-movers if we also constantly blame
others for their existence.

In Jesus' day if you were considered a

'mountain-mover' that meant that you were known as 'a solver of great difficulties.' It has been pointed out that we are known either for the problems we create or the problems we solve. Solving problems eliminates mountains, creating problems builds them. In the Book of Psalms, we are told that the mountains melt like wax at the presence of the Lord; talk about solving or dissolving them; once they melt there is no proof that they even existed.

Elements of Faith – Part Two

Mark 11:24, 25 - Therefore, I tell you, whatever you ask in prayer, believe that you have received it, and it will be yours. And whenever you stand praying, forgive, if you have anything against anyone, so that your Father also who is in heaven may forgive you your trespasses.

Not only will we need to face mountains, remove hindrances and solve problems, but there are going to be many things that we will need to receive from God and then implement in our lives. These are things that we desire from God and even more so; we require from God. That word translated desire is a Greek word that is much stronger than a simple desire; it is a requirement; it is a necessity; we must have it. Like the oxygen in our lungs, it is not an option. Most of our praying is based on a fleeting wish or a vague hope that life could be better; but this kind of prayer that Jesus speaks of springs from an intense desire to fulfil the will of God. We have a destiny and a calling from God; He has designed for us to cooperate with Him in the bringing about of His will and purpose for our lives. He will not overpower us and force His will on us; He wants us to want His will. Jesus teaches us here that for us to receive what God has promised and about which we have asked, we must believe.

What is it that we are to believe? We are to believe that we have received the things desired and asked for. We are to believe that the answer has been given and that we now have it on the inside. Again, this strongly infers that, before our prayer, we have been walking with the Father, and we have been reading the Word of God so that we are intimately acquainted with His will. This kind of faith proceeds from a revelation of security; I know my Father's heart towards me. We do not doubt what He wants for us. We know the will of our Father because we know the Word of our Father. A minister from a previous

century once wrote that faith begins where
the will of God is known. If we do not know
the will of God, we have not yet begun to ask
in faith. First, we must step back and discover
the will of God. Settle the question before we
ask. So, the other thing that we are to believe
is implied; we are to believe that it is the will
of God for us to have the thing that we desire.
At the beginning of verse twenty-four, Jesus
says, therefore; because of what I have
previously said. It is possible that He is
teaching us that because we have been
moving mountains and solving problems, we
are now able to see more clearly what God
desires for us.

Receiving from God is not passive or
automatic; we must be taught how to receive;
we must be informed of the laws of reception.
In football, there is a player who fulfils the
position of a Receiver and it is not a passive
role. The Receiver, must be knowledgeable of
the play-book; he must be well-versed in the
strategies of the team, and then he must
actively get in a position to receive. There are
many similarities to our walk with God;

answers are not automatic; we are required to situate ourselves so that we are in a place to receive. The old Pentecostals used to say, 'You gotta get under the spout where the glory comes out'. The Greek word for receive is also translated take; taking is an action on our part. We are to grasp the answer and take it by faith from the hand of God. God's will to give is subject to His law of reception; it is a transaction between two parties; no giver without a receiver and vice versa.

Right on the heels of some of the most amazing statements and promises in the Word of God, Jesus strategically connects the command to forgive. The reality is that we live in a less-than-perfect world and forgiveness will always be necessary for the maintenance of any relationship. Our relationship to God, our marriage to our spouse, our friendships, and any association with others will require the exercise of forgiveness for that connection to remain healthy. Life is full of disappointment, hurt, difficulty and offences and forgiveness is the only effective antidote to their poison.

To forgive is to let go of whatever we are holding on to or holding against someone. It might be something big, or it might be something small; it matters not; Jesus said 'anything against anybody.' We are not downplaying or making light of the hurt that people have experienced; we have indeed suffered in many ways however, we are commanded to forgive. If I am holding on to something in my hand and I want to get rid of it, I simply let go. That is basically what forgiveness does; it lets go; it removes its grip and releases control. We have all heard the phrase 'Let go and let God' and it certainly applies here. The fact is that forgiveness is not a feeling or emotion per se; it is a choice; it takes a security in God; it takes humility and faith. The day Jesus was crucified he forgave his enemies while painfully hanging from the cross; He released his enemies from their sin, and He released Himself from binding their sin to Himself. A refusal to forgive keeps all parties involved bound to the incident in question. The fact that these words on forgiveness are located where they are it would imply that the biggest hindrance to a robust faith life is an unforgiving spirit.

Father, teach us and empower us to walk by faith and not by sight! Amen!

By Grace Through Faith is the Pattern

Ephesians 2:8, 9 - For by grace are you saved through faith; and that not of yourselves: it is the gift of God: Not of works, lest any man should boast.

In these two verses, I believe that we are given a pattern of the way that we have received and how we can continue to receive from God. By grace through faith is the pattern. Grace made salvation available, and faith made salvation attainable. Grace provided the answer and faith appropriated it. It is not of myself, it is the gift of God. What is the gift of God? I believe that all of it is a gift; the salvation, the grace and the faith. None of this was of my own doing, I did not have grace or faith or salvation within me. It was given to me by a gracious act of God. It is not of works. It is not a result of man's energy or action. Man cannot attain this on his own, it must be given and it must be received. Grace gives, faith receives. Obviously, the grace is not of ourselves. The word grace indicates that another person chose to act a certain way toward us. It is grace; God's choice to love and to provide the solution regardless of our attitude toward him. For grace to be genuine grace it cannot be manipulated or coerced, it must be freely given. Grace is God's attitude toward us, it is his stance and posture. He has the ultimate Father's heart, always thinking of his children. Faith also is a gracious gift enabling us to believe and to receive from him. Without faith I am not able to appropriate what has been provided. Grace offers, faith accepts. Grace delivers the goods, faith signs for it. Grace deposits into the bank, faith withdraws from it. Grace ensures that oxygen is amply available, but faith breathes it in. By grace through faith. Grace made salvation available two thousand years ago when you and I were not here. Quite obviously then, is not of works. Remember that we said that this is a pattern for our continued walk with God. Salvation is the all-inclusive word that gathers into itself all that God intended for us. Healing, deliverance, rescue, safety, preservation and soundness are all included. So we could say it like this; by grace are you healed through faith and that grace, that faith and that healing is not of yourselves, it is the gift of God. By grace are you rescued through faith. By grace are you delivered through faith. By grace we overcome through faith. We don't earn one thing, it is all a gift. God's grace is so big and so vast that he has provided everything and anything that we may need to live a full, productive and satisfying life. It has been made available for you and I; go ahead and receive. By grace through faith. Thank you, Jesus!

A Turn of Events

Philippians 1:19 - For I know that this shall turn to my salvation through your prayer, and the supply of the Spirit of Jesus Christ

Paul is the supreme example of a confident believer. Upon becoming a Christian, his new life immediately became a white-water ride of conflict and trouble, hence, we have Paul writing this letter from a prison cell. Yet, in spite of the trouble, he is confident that God is with him and that nothing has taken God by surprise; he is right in the center of His will. 'I know,' Paul says, 'that this will turn.' He doesn't use unclear language such as I hope this will turn, or it could possibly turn. No! He says, 'I know.' 'I am not upset. I know that God is working behind the scenes, he is influencing and coordinating circumstances and my life is in his hands. My life is not in the hands of my enemies or that of my guards; my life is in the Father's hand, and no man can pluck me out. It might look like I am a prisoner of Rome, but in reality, I am a prisoner of Jesus Christ, captivated by him. I am in the hands of God, being protected and directed accordingly'.

Every circumstance that we find ourselves in, no matter how long it has persisted, is still temporary. It will change. Something will shift. It will turn around. Nothing this side of Heaven will last forever. The tides turn. The seasons turn. The weather turns. Even the Earth itself turns. Paul adds the power of his faith in God to that knowledge and confidently rests, knowing that this story is not over yet. 'This shall turn.' What shall turn? This; this situation; this circumstance; this happening; this occurrence; this challenge; this tragedy; this; this shall turn.

Salvation and deliverance are always the will of God. Jesus came to save us and that is not a one-time deal, no, he saves us daily. He saves us from sin. He saves us from harm. He saves us from our enemies. He saves us from deception. He saves us from ourselves. He doesn't necessarily save us from trouble, but he saves us out of trouble. The Psalmist tells us that, 'Many are the afflictions of the righteous, but the Lord delivers him out of them all.' Everything that we need is answered by the all-encompassing salvation of God. Paul knew the Lord so well that he did not question why he was in prison. He knew that God has ways of working out his will in our lives and he knew that he was there for a reason. The Gospel was actually being proclaimed even more because of Paul's imprisonment. Some of the brothers had taken courage by Paul's stand and were becoming bold and speaking the Word without fear. The whole Roman prison was being influenced for good by Paul's presence there. God is in the salvation business because he is in the people business.

There was another reason that Paul was so confident; he knew that others were praying for him. Oh, how that knowledge can bolster our faith and keep us brimming with hope during the difficult times. This will turn around through your prayer. Paul recognized that he wasn't in this alone but that there was a body of believers praying on his behalf. The word that is used for prayer in this verse is the word that means petition. It is legal terminology. We can petition the court of Heaven and argue, like a lawyer, on behalf of others. The church at Philippi was petitioning God for Paul. Someone has once said that argumentative prayer may be the best kind of prayer. We argue our case before God; we present the facts and the logic and the reason for our petition. The story has been told about the lady whose young daughter was about to be sold into slavery, and she prayed in this argumentative way; 'Lord, if you were in trouble like I am in trouble and I could help you like you could help me, I would do it.' The story as it is told, tells us that after that prayer, someone stepped forward and purchased the child and returned her to the praying mother. This kind of bold praying seems to be a lost art to the modern church; however, a closer look at scripture will reveal its abundant basis. Abraham prayed this way as he negotiated God down to at least ten righteous people in Sodom. Moses prayed this way as he stood in the gap, reasoning with God on behalf of the children of Israel. The Canaanite woman prayed this way when she found some logic to answer the words of Jesus and used his very words to win her case for her daughter. The Centurion prayed this way when he equated his military authority and chain of command to the authority of God's kingdom; thus, logic, reasoning and argument won the answer. All of us likewise must learn to pray this way, presenting our case before God, reminding him of his promises.

Be encouraged, friends, the situation that you are in will turn around for your good. It is the will of God for you to experience his salvation in all of its fullness. God is for you, who can be against you? He is actively working on your behalf and others are fervently praying on your behalf. Get ready, do not despair. This will turn!

What is it That You Want?

Matthew 20:32 – And Jesus stood still and called them and said, What will you that I shall do unto you?

There is something about the nature of Jesus and the way that He works that insists upon us choosing and being specific. The two blind men had just cried out for mercy, and Jesus had heard them. He obviously understood that they wanted mercy but, apparently, mercy comes in drops or showers, and it can cover a lot of ground.

What do you want mercy for? Do you want the mercy that cleanses the soul from any taint of sin that you may have committed? Do you want the mercy that extends compassion toward you in the form of a meal to eat or a place to sleep? Do you want the mercy that lifts you out of the hopeless mindset of the beggar and restores vision and purpose to your floundering soul? Or, do you want the mercy that heals the diseased condition? What is your want? What is your desire?

Mercy is general, but faith is specific. Mercy gets God's attention, but faith gets God's answer. Mercy moves you in God's direction, but faith moves God in your direction. God is a Father who wants to deal with us as mature children. When your adult children want your help, all they have to do is ask. You won't, necessarily, do it for them; you desire for them to honour your relationship by asking. In the book of Exodus when God revealed Himself as, 'I am that I am,' I believe that He is implying that He will be to us whatever we need or desire Him to be, all within the confines of his will, of course. He will meet us on whatever level of faith we are at. Jesus said to the blind men, 'What will ye that I shall do unto you?' I can be a comfort to you in your blindness, or I can be a healer to you of your blindness. I can be a provider to you of your daily needs, or I can bring you to a place of providing for your own needs. I can give you a hand-out that will temporarily satisfy your hunger or I can give you a hand-up that will change your life forever.

It would appear that our choices ultimately determine both the quality and the direction of our life. We may not be responsible for all that has happened to us, but we are in charge of our response. In fact, when we analyze the word responsible, we can see that response is included. Dr. Edwin Louis Cole once said that maturity doesn't come with age; maturity comes with the acceptance of responsibility. If that statement is true, then every time we respond in obedience to God, every time we respond to pressure and difficult situations, we grow; we increase our capacity for handling more; we develop and become more mature.

Whether or not the blind men knew it, when they asked for sight, they asked to become responsible for their lives. They would no longer be looking to others for their sustenance but would become responsible contributors and participants in society.

What are you asking for from the Lord? Please do not misunderstand me; God is so good, and he is way better than we have known; he will bless us in ways that we would never consider doing for ourselves. His mercy will free us from poor choices and neglect, his mercy will rescue us; he is indeed a Saviour. However, there will come a time in our walk with him that he will require us to mature by accepting complete responsibility for our lives. We must stop pointing the finger and blaming others for where we are at, be it our finances, or our marriage, or any area of our life. There are some people who constantly blame others; it's my boss's fault or, my parents or, the government or, my church. Enough of that! What will ye? What do you want? Decide. Choose. Use your power and take action. How long will you hesitate?

Lord, have mercy on us. Give us the mercy that enables us to take charge of our lives and to accept responsibility to cooperate with you in the fulfillment of your will and plan for each one of us. In Jesus' name, I pray, Amen!

Under Authority

Matthew 8:9, 10 - For I am a man under authority, having soldiers under me: and I say to this man, Go, and he goes; and to another, Come, and he comes; and to my servant, Do this, and he does it. When Jesus heard it, he marvelled, and said to them that followed, Verily I say unto you, I have not found so great faith, no, not in Israel.

This account is well known as being the source for many sermons about faith. Jesus commended the Centurion in a way that was quite rare, and it should capture our attention. What was it about this man and the way he conducted himself that so impressed Jesus? As we study the entire passage and the description given to us by Luke, we gain an understanding and a glimpse into the character of this unusual man. We see his humility, we see his compassion, we see his generosity, and we see several other noble character traits; however, it was his faith that Jesus specifically applauded. Jesus did not praise his humility or his compassion or his generosity; he praised and affirmed his faith. There was something so unique and different about this Centurion's faith that Jesus felt compelled to comment; he was amazed; he was impressed. Contrary to some people's thinking, Jesus is not all that easily impressed. Think about it; Jesus had seen it all, he had ministered to the multitudes and dealt with many fascinating people but never had he seen the quality of faith that this man exemplified. What produced this great faith?

We have some insight into the kind of thinking and mindset that created the Centurion's faith by his own comments regarding his understanding of authority. Luke's account gives us a few extra words worth considering. 'I also am a man set under authority.' The Centurion was a military man and he evidently viewed Jesus also as a man, placed under authority like the military. The Centurion understood his place in the chain of command; he was both under men of greater rank, and he was over men of lesser rank. When orders were issued to him, he obeyed without rationale or hesitation; when he issued orders, they were also obeyed. Orders are commands and commands are not suggestions. There are only two responses to a command; obedience or disobedience; we either submit or rebel; we either surrender or resist.

No military man can promote himself; he rises through the chain of command in accordance with his compliance to superior officers and his ability to execute commands. He is set in his rank; he is arranged under others and assigned a particular station. The Centurion became the commander of one hundred men by years of loyal service and experience. There is something about the demeanour of a military man who understands that he is supported by the authority of the nation and also that he carries the authority of the nation. He walks tall; he walks dignified; he walks calmly; he receives orders, and he gives orders; 'Go, come, do this.' These are not requests; they are directives. This Roman officer saw Jesus in the same light. He saw him as being supported and backed by the authority of Heaven. He saw Jesus as being a man who understood his place; he was set there by God. He also saw sickness as something inferior and of lesser rank; Jesus could simply speak a word of command, and the sickness would have to obey, and the servant boy would be healed.

How enlightening and helpful all of this is to us. The greatest commendation and sense of admiration, which ever came from the Lord Jesus, came to a man who was an outsider; a man who the elite religious community would tell us was not welcome or worthy; a man of Rome who was considered an oppressor of Israel; and yet, his understanding of authority transcended all of the above. Great faith is not something to be pursued by us; it is something that is produced in us. It is a consequence of seeing all things in their proper order. Great faith was produced in this man by taking the patterns and methods of his own life and then comparing them to God's way of operating. He did not have to look far to gain this faith; he did not have to work hard to gain this faith; he did not have to burn the midnight oil in study; he simply saw with clarity the way things are from God's perspective. Obviously, that clarity of insight comes from God; we don't unveil these things to ourselves. The Holy Spirit is the revealer of truth, and as we position ourselves to hear from Him, He gives us glimpses and enables us to see and understand the Word of God. When that understanding and insight comes, genuine faith is produced within us; the lies and false perspectives of this world fall away, and we walk forward into our future and into our destiny with confidence and security. Thanks be to God for His unspeakable gift!

God's Statement of Promise

Romans 4:21 - And being fully persuaded that, what he had promised, he was able also to perform.

This statement of Paul comes out of a very powerful section of scripture which describes Abraham and his walk of faith. As we read of the life and the circumstance of Abraham and how he was called by God to pioneer a path of faith for all of us to follow, it is no wonder that he is held in such high esteem all over the world even to this day.

God had spoken to Abraham about the fact that an heir would come out of his own body; he would father his own son. Then God said, 'Look at the stars and count them if you can; so shall your seed be.' That statement is the promise that is spoken of in this verse and in the light of that, we might wish to reconsider our idea of what a promise is. We've heard it said that all of God's promises are conditional; God promises, we meet the condition, and He fulfills the promise. This is our culture's basic understanding of a promise. We do a similar thing with our children; if you clean your room then you can have a snack after dinner; if you do well on your grades then we will buy you a new bicycle. There is certainly an aspect of this that is correct; there is indeed an 'if' in many verses of scripture.

However, let's look closer at this particular promise of God. 'So shall your seed be.' It is not really a promise in the way we normally think of it;it's actually a statement, an announcement or a declaration. This is the way it is. 'So shall your seed be.' As Abraham heard that statement, it produced something in his heart; he became fully persuaded. What was he fully persuaded of? He was completely convinced that what God declared, He was more than able to bring it to pass. This took all of the responsibility right out of Abraham's hands and placed it all exactly where God wanted it; in His hands.

Anybody can make bold declarations, but not everybody can back them up; not everybody has the ability to bring these declarations to pass. Abraham recognized who it was that made the declared promise. God said it; the Creator of the universe was the source of this declaration; God Almighty had spoken, and He is well able to fulfill His promise. Years ago there was a popular saying that went like this, 'God said it, I believe it, and that settles it,' but maybe we should re-phrase it; 'God said it and that settles it.' I believe that this is what happened for Abraham; he heard God speak; he recognized who said it and he fully relied on the character and the ability of the speaker; that settled it.

A man by the name of James Stewart once wrote something which will help us here. He said that 'The constant watchword of the New Testament is not "We are able," but what you do find over and over again is, "He is able," and when [the writers] say it, they are looking away from themselves to God.' God is the one who has all ability, capability, power and might; He is able. We must look away from ourselves and look to Him. This is the persuasive thought that came into Abraham's heart that produced an unshakeable conviction that this promise of God will surely come to pass. What are some of these promises of God for us today? 'All your children shall be taught of the Lord and great shall be the peace of your children', 'By whose stripes you were healed', 'My God shall supply all your need according to His riches'. We are not the performer of these promises; He is. We don't make it happen; God does. We don't have the wisdom to make it happen; we don't have the power to make it happen; we don't have the resources to make it happen; our Heavenly Father does. Our part is simply to accept and agree with what He promises and let that Word persuade us and keep us calm as we lean back in the arms of our Father and allow Him to fulfill His promise. Thank you, Lord! You are definitely more than able!

Notes:

Section Three

<u>Identity</u>

> " *The condition or character as to who a person or thing is; the qualities, and beliefs that distinguish or identify a person or, thing.*

Dictionary.com

What is Your Name?

Luke 8:30 – And Jesus asked him saying, What is your name?

In this account, we have the incident of the man we often refer to as 'The Madman of Gadara'. Most of the teaching that we have heard highlights the fact that Jesus directed His question to the entity that controlled the man, asking the demon, 'What is your name?' However, as true as that may be, G. Campbell Morgan pointed out that perhaps Jesus was, in fact, addressing the man himself, asking him to remember his name. I find this thought to be very inspirational and instructive.

Think of the condition of this poor, tormented man; demon-possessed, self-destructive, anguished, running naked in the cemetery, no life to speak of, no rest, no peace, and no companionships. I am sure that whatever friends and family he may have once had would have been driven away long ago. He is frantic and distressed, but Jesus attempts to snap him out of his frenzy and to rescue him by getting him to remember his name. It seems that recognition and self-acknowledgement of our name becomes our emancipation and liberation from the tormenting powers of darkness.

What is your name? Don't you remember who you are? You were born into a family and your parents lovingly named you. You brought joy and celebration to your father and mother. Recall your youth. You had purpose, dreams, aspirations and friends. Don't you remember? You laughed and played together with the friends of your youth; you fell in love with a beautiful girl; you learned a trade and worked hard providing for your new family.

What is your name? That's who you are. That is your true identity. You are not this raving and tormented lunatic. You are not this violent madman. No! You are a unique individual. You are a person. You are a man, created in the image of God, created to walk

uprightly with dignity, nobility and purpose.
You were destined to engage in society and
contribute to others' success.

What is your name? It is still your name; it
still exists; it may have slipped out of your
memory; the sound of your name may be
vague and faint, but your name has survived.
It's your name, not someone else's. It is
yours; it belongs to you. You matter. You are
missed. You are important. You have a place
in this life. You are a person with a name, and
you are connected relationally to significant
people.

What about us? Have we forgotten who we
are? Have we forgotten our name? Have life's
challenges blurred the memory of our sense of
identity and our personal value and worth?
Have we allowed ourselves to become bitter?
Have we allowed our hearts to become hard?
Have the disappointments and disillusionments
of life created a sense of hopelessness?
Remember who you are. Remember whose
you are and, remember that even though we
may forget, our Father will never forget who

we were created to be. We are living in the days when identity theft has become rampant and it is time to take back our true name. The world has tried to define us and re-name us, but our Heavenly Father has already named us. We are named by God as His very own children and we must never forget who we are. Let this question of Jesus ring loudly in our ears, let it become to us the question that we regularly ask ourselves, and let it spur us forward on our journey through this life. What is your name?

Nothing Insignificant with God

Luke 21:18 – But there shall not a hair of your head perish.

The context of this verse is the persecution and the murder of Christians. Jesus had just finished saying that 'some of you they shall put to death', and then he goes on to say that 'not a hair of your head shall perish.' God's concept and understanding of perishing must be different than ours. When he says not even one strand of hair will perish, then, to him, no matter what comes, even death, that strand of hair still exists. I guess, in the light of quantum physics and sub-atomic particles, then we might be able to say that the hair does indeed still exist. In God's view of things that physical part of you is still there. The resurrection of the physical body bears this out. The body could be in the grave for thousands of years and yet when God says, 'be resurrected', all the particles of the body will come back together to be joined and revived with life. Not a hair on the head of that body has perished.

Of course, he is using hair as an illustration of the smallest part that they could see; he might say, if he were speaking to us today, that not one molecule of your body shall perish. It might have left this physical realm and naturally speaking has perished, but it has not ceased to exist from God's perspective. Whoever believes in Jesus shall not perish but have everlasting life. That word 'shall not perish' goes right through and pervades our entire being; spirt, soul and body; not one aspect of my being shall ever perish.

It is such a powerful thought to understand that God cares for the tiniest things. He cares about that one hair, so to speak. He is a God of amazing detail; he is a master designer that values every microscopic part of his creation. Truly, if we were to say it right, there are no miniscule matters with God. If he created it, then it matters; it cannot be small. The God of the Universe has created every aspect of me and every aspect of my life and, therefore, it teems with significance. He is the creator who has created every facet of my make-up. Just as a manufacturer creates each part with a purpose, so every part in me has particular purpose. Do not believe the lie that insists on your life being meaningless and without eternal purpose and destiny. No! You don't have to search for significance because, by virtue of your existence, you already are infinitely significant. Not one hair of your head shall perish!

Eyes Wide Shut?

Luke 24:31 - And their eyes were opened, and they knew him; and he vanished out of their sight

I remember a season in my life when my eyes were opened to a completely new and exciting world of faith. I was eighteen years old and had just graduated from High School; my life was in chaos because of my many poor choices. There was a period of a few months that I found myself regularly thinking of Jesus and who He was. It seemed that everywhere I looked, even when I didn't want to, I saw signs that pointed me to Him. Little signs that became undeniable to me. My eyes were being opened. This is something that God wants to do for all people. Their eyes are not opened, and so they cannot see Him. Scripture tells us that the 'god of this world has blinded the minds of unbelievers.'

Are your eyes open? Or are your eyes closed? When their eyes were opened, it says that they knew Him. Have you noticed how easy it is to walk through this life with our physical eyes open but not really seeing anything or anyone? With digital technology being so prevalent in our culture, this troubling lack of sight is growing steadily worse. How many times have you driven to work only to arrive there and not remember the drive because your mind was so preoccupied and cluttered with things? It is actually quite scary when you think of it.

The truth is, when it comes to our physical eye, we do not see with the eye, we see in our minds. The eye is simply the organ, the gateway that allows the image in and, then, projects the image on to our minds. That's why we say things like, 'I can see it in my minds' eye'. That is also why you can be looking for an object in your kitchen or, in your garage and it can be right in front of you but you do not see it, because you have a preconceived idea and image in your mind of what it looks like and what it lies next to. The image that you already have formed in your mind clouds the actual sight of your eyes. Your eyes are not open. The disciples were in the very presence of Jesus but until He opened their eyes, they did not know Him, they did not recognize Him. The most recent image that they had of Jesus was of a man who had been brutally tortured by being crucified and put to death. They saw Him tortured. They saw Him die. They saw Him buried. This is what their eyes literally saw; it was very graphically embedded into their minds. So, when something new presented itself, they could not see it, their eyes were not open.

Thank God He opened their eyes. He gave them a different picture and image to focus on. Once their eyes were opened it says that they knew Him and then he vanished out of their sight. The opening of their eyes and the recognition of their Lord gave them a powerfully vivid image to rely upon. They would need it. They were the original pioneers of faith. They would be the ones to first proclaim, to an unbelieving and mocking world, the resurrection of Jesus.

After their eyes were opened, they were able to have a close relationship with the Lord. They knew Him. This is the ancient Hebrew way of describing an intimate encounter of the closest kind. 'Adam knew his wife and she conceived'. This knowledge of Him is not book knowledge; it is heart knowledge, it is not organized knowledge; it is organic knowledge; like the branch knowing the tree; the tree knowing the roots and the roots knowing the soil; it is interconnected and vital knowledge. If our eyes are not opened, we cannot have this type of knowledge.

Shortly after their eyes were opened it says that He vanished out of their sight. Their eyes were opened, they saw Him and now, suddenly, they cannot see Him. He has vanished out of their sight. They saw Him, they rejoiced, they communed with Him and then He quickly departed. I see a pattern of life here in this verse. When our spiritual eyes are first opened there is newness and a freshness of life and joy. We have entered a brand-new world. We have discovered a broad landscape of glorious opportunity. We have met Jesus. We know Him. It is so fulfilling to know Him. It is what we have been created for; to know Him. Usually, not long after our initial encounter and introduction to Jesus, we are introduced to another reality, that of the test of faith. He seemingly vanishes out of our sight. Where did He go? Why did He leave? Can He hear me? Does He see me? Now is the test. Can we walk by faith and not by sight? Can we trust God when we cannot see Him? Can we trust Him in the darkness? Do we understand that this life and our current circumstances are not the only reality and that they are not the strongest reality? He has simply vanished out of our sight; He has not actually vanished. It is all a matter of perspective. Let's make sure that our eyes are open and, having opened eyes, let's take the opportunity and get to know Him better and build our faith, because He will eventually remove Himself from our sight so that we will have the opportunity for a more reliable type of sight to guide us; that of God-given insight.

That was Then, This is Now

Galatians 1:23 - But they had heard only, That he which persecuted us in times past now preaches the faith which once he destroyed.

Paul was an ardent persecutor of the church before he met Christ. He was driven by his religious belief that Christianity was a cult. It was, in his mind, a deception and an affront to faith in Jehovah God. He persecuted anyone that had anything to do with the church. He chased them, hunting them down and dragging them away to prison. When Stephen, the first martyr, was murdered, he stood by in approval. He was convinced that his zeal to destroy the church was of God. He believed that he was doing the will of God by eradicating Christian believers. There is no blindness like religious blindness, and there is no hatred like religious hatred. Paul, known only as Saul then, was definitely not considered by the majority to be a potential believer in Christ. From the outside no one could see that God had his hand on Saul and just as he persecuted and hunted the church, Jesus was ceaselessly tracking Saul. A man by the name of Francis Thompson once wrote a poem entitled, 'The Hound of Heaven' which is a reference to God relentlessly on the hunt, pursuing people to win them and rescue them.

Those early believers were well-aware of Saul. His reputation always preceded him. Once Saul encountered Jesus on the road to Damascus, they began to hear that Saul had dramatically changed. They began to hear that the persecutor of the church was now the protector of the church. He was the bully and the oppressor in times past, but now he is the proclaimer of the faith. He has become the defender of the faith. He is now the church's greatest asset and ally. In times past he was a certain way. That was then, this is now. Everyone has a past of some kind. God is the great intervener of our history. He enters our life and makes the past to become, just that;

the past. That was then, this is now. If Jesus had not revealed himself to us, our past would still be following us into our future; He makes the difference in our story. Before we knew the Lord, we were like Saul; blind, driven and lost, but there has been a divine intervention. Everything has changed because of the grace of God. That was then, this is now!

You Are His Son

Galatians 4:6 - And because you are sons, God hath sent forth the Spirit of his Son into your hearts, crying, Abba, Father.

We are sons of God. What an amazing thought this is. We are sons, we are children of God. We are in the family of God and He is our Father. My wife and I have had the very wonderful privilege of having three sons born into this world. When a little baby is born it does not matter what ones' religious views are, it is undeniably a miraculous event. We are struck with the fact that we have cooperated in the creating of a life and that life is now visible and interacting with its new world. It is a powerful moment in the life of every parent and one that is never forgotten. The day the child was born becomes a day to celebrate for the rest of its life. Why do we celebrate a birthday? We celebrate because that day changed everything. You were born into a family and because you were born into a family you immediately matter; your birth has been recorded and your life is now under the observant and watchful eyes of your parents. There are also certain privileges that come with being a member of the family; such as protection and provision. The little baby has become the sole responsibility of the parents. No one expects this child to care for itself, to the contrary, there has been much planning and provision made for the arrival of this new life. Clothing has been purchased. A room has been prepared. Life is changing for the family by the arrival of a little child.

Paul writes to the Galatians to help them from reverting to a strict and religious, legal relationship with God. He exhorts them to maintain a free and life-giving, family relationship with God. We are sons. We have a Father, and not just any father; we have the Father. We belong to the Father. He has taken responsibility for us and for our provision. He has purchased a new wardrobe, prepared a place and made the necessary provisions for us. If only we could receive it and believe it, we truly would have no worries. Our Father has taken responsibility for our security and our provision. Because we have been born into the family of God, he has sent the Spirit of his Son into our hearts. In order to enjoy the benefits of having a father, we must learn to be sons. A father is a father to his own children only and a son is only a son to his father; it is a living relationship. We have a Father that cares so deeply for us, He sent the Holy Spirit to enable us to walk and live as sons; we have a built-in mentor and guide.

A Clear Voice for God

Luke 3:1, 2 – Now in the fifteenth year of the reign of Tiberius Caesar, Pontius Pilate being governor of Judaea, and Herod being tetrarch of Galilee, and his brother Philip tetrarch of Ituraea and of the region of Trachonitis, and Lysanias the tetrarch of Abilene, And Annas and Caiphas being the High Priests, the Word of God came unto John, the son of Zacharias, in the wilderness.

Luke lists government leaders and spiritual leaders that were contemporaries of John. They were his contemporaries but not, necessarily, his peers. These men were known...John was unknown. These men had a platform...John did not have a platform. These men were recognized authorities...John was not recognized as an authority. These men were included in everyday society...John was excluded and isolated. These men had their own agenda...John was a herald with God's agenda. These men had words...John had the Word. These men had to devise their own words...John had the Word of God come to him.

While life was going on, somewhere behind the scenes, there was a man being prepared by God. He was being prepared to be a voice of God. The Word of God came to John in the wilderness; in the solitary place; in the lonely place; in the isolated and obscure place. We mustn't be afraid of loneliness, isolation or obscurity, for there the Word of God will come to us. He will find us as we wait upon Him. In your wilderness; in your isolation; in your desert place, God's word, God's voice, God's direction, God's wisdom will come to you.

Once we have the word, then we can become a voice. There must be a vocal expression of the word. The word must not be simply spoken to us, but it must be spoken through us. We must become vessels of the word. We must become a voice by which the word of God is transported into the ears of this world. Faith comes to unbelievers as they hear the word spoken. It is a gift of God given to those who hear, through those that speak the words of God.

Let us not be discouraged in our loneliness and isolation. Remember who you are; you came from God. Remember whose you are; you belong to God. He has not forgotten you. Wait on Him, listen to Him, worship Him, yield to Him. For He has enlisted you in the army of believers who come from the spiritual lineage of John; a people who know their God and who are faithful to be the voice of the Word of Life to this generation!

Who Do You Say That He Is?

Mark 8:29 – But whom say ye that I am?

The life Jesus lived on Earth, though quite short, has had and continues to have, an innumerable and unsurpassed influence on this world. He made a lasting impact on all those that came in contact with Him. His name, His words, His demeanour, and His miracles stirred up an immense amount of interest and piqued the curiosity of a nation. There were diverse and assorted opinions of Him. Jesus had just asked His disciples what some of those opinions were. Who did people say He was? Some, apparently, said that He was the forerunner, John the Baptist, raised from the dead. Others said He was Elijah, the confrontational prophet who challenged the false religion of his day. Then there were those who thought he resembled Jeremiah, the one who felt the pain of Israel's condition and wept over the people of God. A large number of things were said about Him. Some people loved Him and some despised Him. Some gave their all to Him in worship and others tried to use Him for their gain. Many were impressed with His wisdom and teachings and there were also those who thought He had lost His mind and was insane. Without fail, the mention of Jesus never left anyone the same. He became a controversial figure, a person about whom many rumours and false truths were circulated. There were a multitude of opinions about Him then and there are equally as many about Him now. However, it really does not matter what the world says about who Jesus is. It does not matter what the current view of Him is, it only matters what you and I believe personally.

Who do you say that I am? Jesus' question is not simply for those to whom it was first posed but it is for each of us today. It is a personal question. It is a penetrating question. It is a probing question. It is a paramount question that has eternal ramifications. It is a question that demands an answer. Who do I say that He is? Who is He? The question is not what Jesus has done for me, although He has done so much, the question is who do I say He is? Eternity rests not on what but on whom; not on a thing but on a person; not on a system but on a Saviour. Who is He? We have no doubt heard the phrase that it is not what you know but who you know that counts. This idea suggests that to get the right opportunities and to get ahead in life depends not upon your education or your skills but upon who you are in relationship with. It is not what but who. When we apply this thought to Christianity it actually rings true. I may have all kinds of knowledge, even a thorough Biblical knowledge and yet not truly know Jesus. There are those who even have positions of leadership in churches and other organizations but may not necessarily know Him. A relationship is not based on what you know about someone. I may know many things about a movie star or a famous athlete. I might be able to quote their list of films and maybe even know their career stats but never actually met them. Who a person is, not what a person does, is the essence of relational intimacy. I can learn much about a person indirectly but I can never learn who a person is second hand. It must be a first hand and face to face encounter.

The question searches even deeper than simply recognizing who He is; it asks us to say something. What do I say of Him? What do I say to Him? What do I say to myself? What do I say to others? It is not enough to merely think about who He is; there must be a statement. If someone witnesses a crime and then reports it to the police, the police will require a statement. If two people are deeply in love and decide to get married, the love alone will not suffice; the minister will require a statement. We are committed to what we confess. Christianity has been called The Great Confession and rightly so because it is based on a verbal statement of your faith in Jesus. Words are the formulation and expression of what is in our hearts. When our children are struggling or hurting, we want them to have the freedom to say what it is that is bothering them. When a counsellor is trying to get to the root of inner trouble, they need to hear what is in the heart. Many times, the simple act of saying something out loud takes it out of the vague and gives it tangible meaning. This applies to both the negative and the positive. Stating things verbally not only brings solutions to problems but it also enhances and strengthens our faith and our love. I tell my wife that I love her not only because she needs to hear it but because I need to hear it; it reinforces my love and adds power to my commitment. Jesus knew this about human nature. He knew those first disciples would need to have a strong commitment in order to pioneer and forge a path for succeeding generations and He knew that we would, likewise, need much help in our journey through life and in our walk with Him.

Who is He? Who do you say He is? Who do I say He is? I say that He is the Christ. He is the Son of God. He is the Saviour of the world. He is the Lord of all, and He is my Lord and Saviour. He is my Redeemer and Rescuer. He is the Beautiful and Worthy One. That's who He is and that's my statement! Who do you say that He is?

His Plan, Our Purpose

2 Timothy 1:9 - Who hath saved us, and called us with an holy calling, not according to our works, but according to his own purpose and grace, which was given us in Christ Jesus before the world began

God has saved us, that is, He has rescued us, delivered us, and brought us into a place of safety. Thank you, Lord, for this salvation. God is the original 'Search and Rescue' team; He is ever seeking and ever desiring to rescue people from danger and destruction and to bring them to a place of protection and wellbeing. It is impossible to rescue those who don't believe that they need rescuing; so our first prayer for all those who do not know the Lord would be one that would open their eyes to the vital need that they have. We do not save or rescue ourselves, in fact, if you were in a tight situation and you got yourself out of it, you would never refer to that as being rescued; you may instead boast of how you got out of that hazardous place by your own strength and ingenuity. Being rescued implies a Rescuer, a Saviour; someone other than yourself and someone stronger than yourself who has come alongside of you to help.

Not only has God saved us but He has also called us; He has spoken and voiced His desire for us to respond to the call and come to Him. Years ago, as children, playing in the orchards behind our house, we would hear the call to dinner. Once the call was given it was then incumbent upon us to respond and to come and seat ourselves at the table. If we went hungry because we did not respond to the invitation that could never be our parents' fault. A call is something that another must initiate; we can never call ourselves. If you were informed at the office that you have a call holding on the line, at the very least it would be rude not to answer the call. It may also be very foolish because the one who is calling could be a person of great wealth and ready to purchase your wares. These

examples of earthly calls pale in comparison to the Heavenly call; God, Himself, has called us, and that call is a call to fellowship and partnership with Him. It is also a call to holiness, which is a life set apart for use by Him. It is a sacred calling. It is a special calling. Indeed, it is a noble calling.

I once heard someone describe the tour that they took through a museum where they were shown Abraham Lincoln's desk and office paraphernalia. The curator of the museum informed the visitors that the artefacts were extremely valuable and even the pen of Abraham Lincoln was worth a vast amount of money. Granted, the pen was simply an ordinary pen, it was not made of gold or special and rare jewels. It was not valuable because of the pen itself; it was valuable and even priceless because of the one who used it. The call of God is a call to be used by Him, to become an instrument of blessing in His hands. In the light of who is using the instrument, His call adds a great deal of value to our lives.

The idea of a call or a calling needs to be scripturally re-examined. We have often heard it used in reference to those who are ordained ministers or to those who have a full-time job in ministry type work; indeed, they do have a calling. However, the Scripture is very clear that all people are called. If we believe that He has saved us, all of us, then we must likewise believe that He has called us, all of us. All people have a unique and essential calling. Just as the members of our bodies do not all have the same function, yet all are absolutely designed with a unique purpose that another cannot fulfil.

God initiated a relationship with us; He made the first move; He pursued us. The reason that He pursued us was not because we had an amazing track record of impeccable living, or that we had so much to offer; No! His call was not according to our works. None of our good works would qualify us and equally so, none of our sinful works could disqualify us. It was not because of our actions or our efforts, it was initiated because He had a purpose for us, and He wanted to instill His destiny in our lives. He called us, He chose us, and He had a plan. God had a purpose for each one of us, He intended for us to enjoy great fulfilment and a life of accomplishment and satisfaction by aligning ourselves with His purpose. However, He also foreknew that we would not naturally or, automatically walk in that purpose so He ensured that we also have His grace which empowers and enables us to follow His purpose and plan. God's grace is too vast to define but one aspect of it is His willingness to use His resources on our behalf regardless of our personal merit.

All of this; His salvation, His calling, His purpose and His grace was all given to us before the world began. God in His perfect foreknowledge saw that mankind would fall and would need redemption. Even before there was a problem God provided the answer, in fact, there is no problem that His answer won't meet. It was all decided upon ages ago; before the creation of man; before the rebellion of man; it was given freely to all of us in the person of His Son; it was given to us in Christ Jesus. Thank you, Father God, for the origin of the plan. Thank you, Jesus, for the execution of the plan and, thank you, Holy Spirit, for the unveiling of the plan. Oh! What purpose we have and what grace we've been given!

Behind Closed Doors

Luke 24:16 – But their eyes were held that they should not know Him.

This incident takes place shortly after the resurrection of Jesus. Two of His followers encountered Jesus as they were on the road to another town, but they did not recognize Him. They walked together and talked of the events of the previous few days and all the while they still did not realize that it was Jesus who was speaking with them.

This phrase, 'their eyes were held', is a figure of speech which is very instructive. Did God hold their eyes from seeing Jesus? It certainly is possible for he has done it before. I remember reading an account of people who were smuggling Bibles into a country where Christianity was outlawed. The border guards opened their luggage and even looked directly into the compartment where the Bibles were hidden; they looked right at the Bibles but did not see them; apparently, God held their eyes.

Another way of looking at this is to consider that we are the ones who close our own eyes. The original writings tell us that their eyes were held, that is they were fixed or seized. Something had previously captured their attention. They had just recently watched as Jesus was brutally tortured and crucified. They watched Him die, they saw Him buried, and now their eyes were fixated on that and unable to see anything else.

How many times has this happened to us? Something terrible happens to us and it makes a deep impression on our minds and from that point on we are not able to see anything but that incident. We might have lost a loved-one; can we see ourselves being happy again? We might have experienced a financial crisis; can we see ourselves recovering from it? We might have been betrayed by our spouse; can we see ourselves being able to trust again? We might have failed in ministry; can we see ourselves being used of God again? These things are real and all of us deal with it; we must deal with loss and sorrow for we are the ones who are in charge of our own minds. Can we open up and see again?

Closed eyes can also imply a hardened heart; a decision to not be open or vulnerable again; a choice to close off the possibility of new and exciting things. If we remain in a seized state, fixated on the past, we can never really know Him; we thus close ourselves off from intimacy with God and others. Closed eyes mean a closed mind; a closed mind means a closed heart; a closed heart means a closed life. Consequently, we shut ourselves away from hope; we lock ourselves behind closed doors in a room with no light, sentencing ourselves to solitary confinement.

Take courage, friends, we are in this together and our Father God is in the door-opening business. It matters not where we have locked ourselves away, or for how long; He will keep seeking us out and drawing us back until we give Him the key to the door of our life. Hear Him whisper His word to you today, and even though the room may be dark, and your eyes cannot see, we believe it shall be as the Book of Psalms says, 'Your word is a door that lets in light.'

Notes:

Section Four

Character

" The condition or character as to who a person or thing is, the qualities, and beliefs that distinguish or identify a person or, thing.

The attributes and features that make up and distinguish an individual.

Merriam-Webster

Are You Building to Last?

Matthew 7:24 – 27 - Therefore whoever hears these sayings of mine, and does them, I will liken him unto a wise man, who built his house upon a rock: And the rain descended, and the floods came, and the winds blew, and beat upon that house; and it fell not: for it was founded upon a rock. And every one that hears these sayings of mine, and does them not, shall be likened unto a foolish man, who built his house upon the sand: And the rain descended, and the floods came, and the winds blew, and beat upon that house; and it fell: and great was the fall of it.

Jesus contrasts two different people; the wise and the foolish. Many times, when we read this, we mistakenly assume that Jesus is talking about believers and unbelievers. A closer examination, however, tells us that Jesus is speaking to believers. Unbelievers are not sitting at the feet of Jesus hearing his teaching. So, this instruction and warning is for all of us as believers. Which type of man will I be? Will I be wise or foolish? I, alone, am in charge of that choice.

The wise man built his house on the rock, so the question arises, 'What is the rock?' Most believers respond to that question by saying that the rock is God. It is true that in the book of Psalms, God is known as the Rock of our salvation; our steady, unchanging, always reliable and permanent security. However, in this verse, God is not the rock upon which the wise man built his house. The rock is his personal application and consistent practice of the words that he heard; it is the bending of his will to the Lord and the forming of his integrity. He did not simply hear but he acted on the word of God, thus constructing his life and character on the security and permanence of eternal foundations.

Apparently, wisdom and knowledge are not

the same thing. Both men heard the words of Jesus, so they both had knowledge, but only one had wisdom. Knowledge alone does not guarantee that we are building securely; in fact, we could be building on shifting sand, all the while quoting Bible verses. In contrast, wisdom is always looking way down the road ahead. Wisdom plans and builds for the future, even peering into the distance and preparing for eternity. The wise man did not take the easy route by digging a foundation in loose soil; no, he took the harder route by digging deep and chipping into the rock, slowly laying his foundation in the bedrock of faithfulness. We can imagine that the foolish man's house seemed to be making better progress; he had his roof on before the wise man was finished with his foundation. In our fast-paced, get-it-done-now culture, slow and steady progress may be just what we need.

Both men heard the word of God and built their lives; one by commission and diligence; the other by omission and negligence. From the outside both houses looked the same; it was only in the hidden realm that there was an infinite difference; and it was only when the storm came that the difference was revealed. The storms of life will inevitably come to all of us, at various intervals of our lives, and wise is the one who foresees such storms. Wisdom is not taken by surprise, but foolishness always is. A fool continues to build on the sand, presuming that no storm will come, and even if it does, he seems to think his house will stand.

I have heard it said that in one Oriental language there is only one symbol that stands for both crisis and opportunity. When the troubles and the tests come it reveals our character and it is our character that predetermines whether it will be a crisis causing our lives to crash or whether it will be an opportunity causing our resolve to be strengthened by God. Dr. Edwin Louis Cole once wrote, "There are no spur-of-the-moment decisions, but every decision is based on a lifetime of previous decisions which either enhanced or diminished one's character".

I pray that we would awaken to a deeper

resolve to continue to build on the firm foundation. If we have sinned and made mistakes, as all of us have, then make this an opportunity to repair the faulty foundations and get back on a path of wisdom; building the unseen life one brick at a time. It will be worth it!

Passing Tests, or Learning?

*Ephesians 4:20 - But you have not so
learned Christ*

Much is said in Paul's writings about
revelation and how he experienced a dramatic
and personal unveiling of Jesus. The Lord
revealed himself to Paul. Later Paul was
caught up into the third Heaven and was given
abundant revelation; insight and
understanding that was imparted to him
instantaneously. Revelation is instantaneous
but learning is a process. Paul had both
revelation and a process of learning in his life.
The Ephesians also apparently, learned Christ.
They were taught and they acquired
knowledge over a period of time. Learning is
all important to life. Children must not just be
taught, they must learn. We do not want to
pass a child into the next grade because they
were simply in the same classroom as
everyone else and heard all the same

teaching. No! Did the child learn? Sadly, our culture has given us the wrong impression. We have been taught to pass tests instead of learn. We emphasize the passing of the test, so we cram for the exam, and because it is fresh on our minds, we can remember the necessary answers and obtain a passing grade. The answers were in our mind, but not in our life. If we learn what we need to learn, the passing of the test will be a consequence, not a goal. Learning and developing in character and skill should be the goal; passing the test and getting the good grade will be the result.

Let's apply that to our walk with God. We are not to simply pass tests or even acquire information. We might be able to quote multiple verses of Scripture, but that is no guarantee that we have learned. Learning is the discipleship word. We are not just a pupil, but an apprentice. If we think like that, we will get a better picture of what God wants for us. He wants us to not simply have book knowledge, or head knowledge, but he wants us to be trained as apprentices so we can acquire the necessary skills to succeed. We must learn Christ. We must learn him, which means that we learn a person. When you associate closely with a person, you eventually take on the characteristics, attitude and habits of that person. Jesus had said to his disciples earlier, 'Take my yoke upon you and learn of me.'

Just as it is necessary to learn Christ, it is also important how you learn. Paul said that they 'had not so learned' Christ. They had not learned Christ in the same manner in which some others had learned. We must be true to the way that the Lord has led us and the methods by which that He has taught us. In what manner have you learned Christ? Obviously, we are open to more learning and to different ways of learning, but it is important that we honour our roots. Honour those who have shown you the way of the Lord. Honour the history of your walk with God by continuing to learn from it. God knows us. He knows exactly how to speak to us and how to deal with us so that we may learn and thereby be changed and experience greater levels of freedom. Every parent and schoolteacher knows that each child is different and has a unique way of learning, and our walk with Christ is a lifelong process of learning. As we grow and mature, he teaches us a little more, and shows us another aspect of his character and grace.

There are tests in life and there are things that we face that are very difficult, for sure. However, let's be sure to not simply go through the experience, but let's be sure to learn. We sometimes have heard it said that experience is the best teacher, but if that were true wouldn't we all be a lot smarter? Experience is important, but learning something from your experience is more important. So, the next time that you are in a pressure situation, be sure to learn Christ in the middle of it all, take on His attitude and characteristics, and be changed into the same image by His power and by His grace.

Motive is Everything

2 Corinthians 7:12 - Wherefore, though I wrote unto you, I did it not for his cause that had done the wrong, nor for his cause that suffered wrong, but that our care for you in the sight of God might appear unto you.

Paul had written some very strong things to the Corinthians in his previous letter, and they received the instructions and carried them out. This godly leader helps us to see that motives are extremely important. He did not write to them to take up the cause of someone who had suffered wrong; we would call that 'taking up someone else's offense.' Paul emphatically states that he did not write with that motive. The injustice of what happened is not what drove him. Nor did he write for the purpose of punishing the wrong doer; because they deserved to pay for it. No! He wrote to them, motivated by a deep love and a compelling desire for them to see the profound care that God had put in his heart.

How instructive this is for leaders today. It is so easy to allow the inevitable issues and troubles in the church to be the driver behind all that one does. Heart intentions are what God ultimately sees; the purposes and reasons which are the roots of our actions. Man looks on the outward appearance, but the Lord looks on the heart; the Lord weighs the spirits. The deep motives within us are what God sees and deals with. Even our court systems will hand out a harsher sentence for someone who had pre-meditated motives and the system will be more lenient on someone who did not have a wrong intention.

As leaders, parents, or employers we must be prayerful and honest when addressing the actions of others. Why am I addressing this? Am I trying to appear just and fair? Am I simply doing the right thing? Am I upset with the person who did the wrong, or am I sympathizing with the one who has been wronged?

One of the major problems, in dealing with these issues on our own, is that we are limited in our perspective. We only see what has happened, or maybe what we have heard; we do not see the complete picture. Paul's intention, in writing to the Corinthians and addressing the situation, was that they would see that it was God's love that compelled him.

Someone has once written that there are three things that need to be right; the message, the method and the motive. Our message is the Word of God. If we keep that in the forefront the message will always be right. Methods will usually vary and are adjusted to each situation. Every parent knows that each child and each situation must be dealt with separately. What worked with one child and situation may not work on the next. The method may have to change. The message never changes, the methods can and probably should change, however, underlying all of it must be the motive. I can have the right message with a correct method, and it can still turn out very poorly, because I may not have had the proper motive. Before bringing the correction, or making a change in your family, or your organization be sure to ask yourself the hard question; why am I doing this; what is my motive?

It is important that we emphasize that we are talking about judging our own motives, not those of another. When we begin to judge the deep motives and intentions of others, we are treading on sacred ground that only belongs to God. He is the only one who can truly judge the heart. As we take the time to reflect and consider these things, the answer will come to us; the Lord will show us our true motives and we will be able to make the adjustments and apply the wisdom shown to us. This is the hidden key to success in any enterprise; always be careful and maybe even a little bit suspect of your underlying intentions; indeed, motive is everything.

We Spend Time; Can We Also Buy It?

Ephesians 5:16 - Redeeming the time, because the days are evil.

Have you noticed how driven we are by time? Our alarms go off at a certain time in the morning. We get dressed and ready so we can make it to work on time. We spend the day keeping appointments which are set for specific times. Most of our life revolves around a time schedule. We plan our exercise program so we can be fit after we invest some time at it. We save our money so it can build over time. We raise our children knowing that the time will come when they are on their own. Time, time, time; it is the one thing that all of humanity shares. We all have twenty-four hours in a day. All people, young and old, rich and poor, regardless of their culture, status, or beliefs have this one thing in common; we only have so much time.

Someone once said that time is really the only resource we have. We exchange time for everything else. The word itself is used in an economic fashion; we spend time.

Paul says that we are to redeem the time. Redeem is an interesting and picturesque word because it means to buy up, or rescue from loss. Like a merchant who eagerly buys up a scarce commodity; we are to buy up the opportunities presented to us. There are also two ways to look at the concept of time. There is chronological time; the kind that marches on and waits for no man, and there are strategic seasons and points of opportunity which quite often come unexpectedly. The Greeks called these opportunities 'kairos' moments and this is the word that Paul uses. Most of these moments arise unpredictably and usually are brief and fleeting. They come and they go, like the water that passes under the bridge, in truth, it never comes around again. These times may include such things as the birth of a child, a morning sunrise, a tender kiss, or kind words from a stranger. However, kairos moments also come at times of crisis. I remember a friend of mine telling me that, in a certain oriental language, their one word for crisis meant both danger and opportunity. When the crisis of life comes, it is a time of danger, but it is also an opportunity for positive and powerful change. We are exhorted by Paul to redeem the opportunity; to not let it pass us by, but to make the most of it. There are times in our life when the Lord is speaking to us and we know that it is him speaking. That is the time; the kairos moment which is the opportunity that is presenting itself. Stop and purchase that opportunity; stop and smell the roses, so to speak. Isaiah said to 'seek the Lord while he may be found, call upon him while he is near.' In other words, redeem the time; buy the opportunity.

When Paul uses the phrase 'because the days are evil', I believe he means that because of the fall of man, life does not automatically promote good things, therefore the time needs to be redeemed. Just as your garden will not automatically produce good and healthy vegetables without your active cooperation, so our lives need our awareness to make the most of every opportunity. Thank God that we can, by his grace, redeem the time!

There Will Always be Another King

Acts 7:18 - Till another king arose, which knew not Joseph.

There will always be another king. One of the tendencies of humanity is that we cannot seem to see very far in front of us, and we are also inclined to forget what has happened behind us on the road of history. The stark reality is that we are on this earth for a short season and inevitably succession will come. Nothing in this life lasts forever. Every championship team knows that it is one thing to obtain the status of champions, and a whole other thing to maintain it. Just because you won last season does not mean it will happen automatically, again this season. The hunger of the challenging team will drive them on in a relentless pursuit of the title. There will always be another king. Successful companies understand that they may be at the top of their industry one year, but that is no guarantee that they will repeat their performance again and they may even find themselves struggling the following year. Competition is fierce in the modern business world and new and improved companies and products are being launched every minute. There will always be another king.

The verse we are looking at is describing the experience of the children of Israel in Egypt. God gave Joseph favour and wisdom with Pharaoh, king of Egypt, and he was promoted into high levels of influence and responsibility. Both the Egyptians and the Israelites enjoyed a season of prosperity and blessing under this king because of his honourable relationship with Joseph. But another king arose who did not know Joseph. That king, apparently, did not value the history that Egypt had with Joseph and the Israelites. He did not acknowledge the fact that there were others who had helped him get to this place of power. He did not know Joseph. There is a popular phrase that says 'It's not what you know but who you know that counts', and we sometimes laugh at that idea, but the truth is, entrance into heaven isn't based on what you know, but on who you know. Who you know is all-important and has eternal ramifications. Who you know, who you honour, who you acknowledge, and who you associate with, will determine your destiny. Sadly, this new king did not know Joseph.

Another king arose. This other king had a different spirit than the previous one had. He didn't have a reverence for God and for his people. He did not have a compassionate heart, but, obviously, had a self-serving motive. He was a king of another type than his predecessor. Arrogant pride is persistent; it lurks in the shadows, waiting for an opportunity to destroy each one of us. Prideful conceit is the ever-constant enemy of mankind and it is cunningly deceptive by nature. We are deceived when we forget or don't even acknowledge that many people have sacrificed their lives, their time, their money, their energy; all for someone else's benefit; all for my benefit. I live in a city which has roads and power and a water system; all of which I enjoy the use of but did not contribute to any of it. It was all built before I was born, and I must look back to appreciate what others have done for me. I may be sitting in a beautiful church auditorium with my family, enjoying and benefiting from the numerous ministries of the church, and never whispering even one prayer of gratitude for all those who sacrificed to build it. We don't want to be like this other king, who chose to ignore the hard work done by his forbearers long before he rose to power.

Someone has once commented that there are, in the scripture, more commands to remember than any other command. Scripture exhorts us, again and again, to not forget but, to remember. Remember those who have spoken to you the word of God, remember those who are in prison, remember that it is the Lord God who gives you the power to get wealth, remember Lot's wife, remember that you were once a slave, remember your history, and remember God's faithfulness. Another king will always arise, but will he remember? More importantly, will we remember?

The Christian Life is to be Continued

Acts 14:22 - Confirming the souls of the disciples, and exhorting them to continue in the faith, and that we must through much tribulation enter into the kingdom of God.

Paul and Barnabas had both tremendous success and remarkable opposition on their first missionary journey. They had to flee at times, being literally chased out of cities; Paul himself was unjustly and brutally stoned to the point of death. These men were definitely not self-focused or self-centred men. They were men motivated by both the Spirit of God and the charge that they were given, as they were sent by God to this region. Even after pouring themselves out during an intense time of hostility to their ministry, instead of being the ones looking for attention and seeking sympathy, they were the ones who were supporting and reinforcing others. After being driven out of several cities, they went directly back in to those very same cities to bring encouragement and strength to the disciples.

Our text tells us that Paul and Barnabas confirmed the souls of the disciples. Whatever they said to them, it strengthened their soul; it fortified their inner life, it encouraged their mental state and emotional perspective. The battle that we face daily is, primarily, spiritual. It is not a physical battle of wit or weapons, neither is it a conflict of brain or brawn. We are not going to win in a fight of mere intellect, nor will we succeed in a contest of sheer muscle. No! Even though we have much outward opposition, our real struggle is nonphysical, invisible, and keenly personal. It is a battle of the soul.

Probably the first thing that we will encounter as a believer is the temptation to quit, acquiescing and surrendering our faith. This tactic of temptation is aimed at your soul, that is, your mind, your will and your emotions. You may begin to rationalize your situation and attempt to reason your way out of continuing this way of faith. If we are continuing in the faith, then, that means that we are staying in the place of faith. The fight is intended to get us to move out of the place of faith that we already occupy. Paul says elsewhere to 'fight the good fight of faith'; it is a fight to remain steady under intense pressure to quit.

As believers, we must realize that the enemy we face is a clever strategist and an experienced psychologist. He has been studying methods of warfare and the habits of mankind for over 6000 years. Remember, we are not going to win in a fight of mere intellect; we are not going to outsmart the devil, however, we can outlast him. As one old prophet-preacher used to say, 'Perseverance will always outlast persecution.'

Paul and Barnabas came back to those new believers and exhorted them to continue holding their ground. The word exhort is very descriptive; it pictures the leader of an army coming to the frontline where his battle-weary troops are assembled. He stands before them and exhorts them; he summons them to look deep within their hearts and to remember why they are fighting. 'Think of your country, think of your family, think of your freedom and ride forth with me into victory. We can do this and together we shall conquer!' The enemy is like the criminal invaders of an army; he is trying to take what the people of the land already have. You and I are citizens of Heaven's land, we are not trying to attain the ground; we are simply defending what the Lord has already given to us. As fellow believers we need to constantly exhort one another. 'You can do this! Christ in you is sufficient! The Greater One indwells you and he is causing you to stand your ground! We will prevail if we do not surrender and forfeit our authority.'

I want to encourage you today. You may be going through the battle of your life, but remember, that the battle of today is not just about today; it is about your future and eternal destiny. Also, this fight is not just about you; it is about those around you; family, friends, and others who are looking to you and secretly hoping that your Jesus is indeed real and that he has the answers for them as well. God is with you and he has committed himself and all of heaven's resources to see you succeed. The key to victory is wrapped up in one word: continue.

Post a No Vacancy Sign

Matthew 12:43-45 -   When the unclean spirit is gone out of a man, he walks through dry places, seeking rest, and finds none. Then he says, I will return into my house from whence I came out; and when he is come, he finds it empty, swept, and garnished. Then he goes and takes with himself seven other spirits more wicked than himself, and they enter in and dwell there: and the last state of that man is worse than the first. Even so shall it be also unto this wicked generation.

Quite often when we read this portion of scripture, we relegate it only to those poor souls who have been demon possessed and completely taken over, but there is unique insight and powerful principles here for all of us to consider and learn.

Firstly, we can see the nature of the enemy in that he is a restless entity; ever seeking, never finding; an eternal vagabond, acutely aware of a gnawing sense of endless agitation. That is Satan's disposition and that sensation is what he attempts to foster in the heart of man. If you have ever had any acquaintance or dealings with an unsettled and restless person, you know that it is seems almost futile to help them; true rest can only come from above, and only a restful person has genuine authority and lasting victory over the adversary.

Another thing that we see with respect to the nature of the enemy is that he desires to own, possess and occupy man. He is ever seeking to influence, manipulate and control whomever he can; accordingly, then, the enemy, once dealt with, must continue to be dealt with. We can exercise authority and cast him out but, subsequently, we must exercise vigilance and keep him out. The enemy desires to return and to come back into the same place that he once ruled, and because he is a persistent opponent, watchfulness and attentiveness are some of the necessary elements that will secure our continued freedom.

Not only does the unclean spirit want to return but, he wants to reinforce his previously held stronghold; bringing the man into a worse state than the first. So again, we get a glimpse into his strategy and tactics. The enemy has an intention to strengthen his wicked purpose and ultimately bring utter devastation and ruin to the man. Make no mistake friends, there is a war and we are the targets; our foe hates all that even remotely resembles the image of God in man. We may have met some harsh, hard-hearted people but they pale in comparison with just how malicious, menacing and cruel this evil spirit truly is.

When the unclean spirit had the rule of the house, disorder and uncleanness was the norm. Once that spirit was gone the man was able to clean up his life and set things in order, however that is not enough. Any house, even if it is in a posh neighbourhood, must be occupied to ensure its safety and maintenance. Thieves love to find clean, orderly and vacant houses, because unoccupied houses have no one home to defend them. The problem with this house was not that it was clean and orderly, the problem was that it remained empty. There is an old saying that tells us that nature abhors a vacuum, but so also does the human heart; something will inevitably fill it.

The principle we are being taught here is what we might call the Law of Displacement. When the children of Israel were commanded to go in and possess the Promised Land, the first thing they had to do was deal with the occupants of the land; they had to drive out the enemy. Once the enemy had been driven out, he was to be kept out by their occupation of the new land, in other words, they displaced the enemy. We could also describe this law another way; how would one get the air out of a glass? You couldn't shake it out. You could turn the glass upside down but, still the air would not come out. The only way to get air out of a glass and keep it out, is to fill the glass with another substance, such as water. The water, then, displaces the air and prevents its return.

Holy Spirit, please come and fill our hearts with your presence, fill our minds with your thoughts and fill our lives with a renewed sense of purpose. Let this next season be one of an awakening to all that God has for us. Let us be filled, be focused and remain free, in Jesus' name, amen!

Old, Strong and Productive

Acts 21:16 - There went with us also certain of the disciples of Caesarea, and brought with them one Mnason of Cyprus, an old disciple, with whom we should lodge.

Only the Word of God could use a simple phrase from an obscure verse to teach unending lessons and powerful truths. While reading this verse, two words spring to life; old disciple.

Our world, with its never-ending fight against aging, and its perpetual quest for the fountain of youth, certainly does not value the old. Even the very mention of the word conjures up images of decrepit things; an old car, dented and rusty, burning more oil than gas; an old house, with a leaking roof and weathered siding, that has long since become a bottomless money-pit; or maybe, an old computer; with its out-dated technology demonstrated by memory measured in kilobytes and containing a floppy drive. However, in God's economy, old never means decrepit and worn out; it means time-tested, valued, seasoned and so much more.

Our culture worships the new; be it a new car, a new philosophy, new hair or, a new mate. And lest we should point our finger at society, the Christian church has not fared much differently; we seem to always want the new, as well. We want new songs with new instruments because the old ones were those of our parents. We want new books with bright new covers because the old ones were much too plain. We want new ambience complete with modern lighting and decor because the old just wasn't attracting others to our assembly. Don't misunderstand me, I do believe that methods and tools need to be updated, but new, for the sake of new, is not wise. Many years ago, I read a quote from G. K. Chesterton which went something like this; 'Weak things must boast of being new, but strong things can boast of being old.'

In the light of that quote, our man named Mnason, wasn't simply an old disciple, he was vastly more; he was a strong disciple. He was old and strong like the tree with roots reaching deep into the soil, absorbing the much needed nutrients, while simultaneously maintaining stability and ensuring permanence. He was old and strong like the river whose waters bring life to living things, while carving and shaping a path for succeeding generations to follow. He was old and strong like the buildings and bridges which were constructed in times past; built to last, using materials that were proven to weather the harsh storms of life and stand tall as a testimony to the architect.

Scholars tell us that this word old, in the Greek language, means original, and according to several commentators this could very well imply that Mnason was one of the original disciples who lived as a contemporary of Jesus. We can imagine the possibility of him being one of the many who sat and listened to the life, changing truths contained in the Sermon on the Mount. Maybe he was there that day as the woman pushed through the crowd and touched the garment of Jesus receiving healing and restoration of dignity and purpose, or perhaps he was present when the outcast leper came and asked for the touch of Christ and was mercifully cured and reunited with family and friends. If only we had eyes that were opened to see the old disciples, like Mnason, sitting among us; what stories we might hear; what lessons we might learn; what impact we might experience.

Not only is our brother said to be old, but he is noted also, as a disciple. An old disciple. Some people simply grow old, but they do not do it gracefully. Many times, they grow old and bitter, or old and despondent, or old and more prejudiced than ever. We value long life, but we don't want to simply live for a long time, we want to continue on the path of a disciple. We have many believers in Christ, but relatively few disciples of Christ. A disciple is a student; one who remains engaged and active, continually learning, perpetually growing, and consistently giving. The outward man is perishing and aging, but the inward man need not diminish but can be renewed daily.

Paul, himself an old disciple, wrote to Titus and instructed him to speak to the older men and women of Crete, reminding them to finish strong. Wisdom is cumulative and spiritual power can actually amass as we walk with the Lord through our youth and into our fifties, sixties, seventies and eighties. Experienced disciples become extremely valuable to God and others; hence the exhortation to the older ones. Leaders need to remind the older generation, encouraging them to not forget how valuable they are as they age. We are not to take our identity from what the world says about us, we must get our identity from God; we must remember who we are; remember whose we are; and remember who is looking toward us for hope and support. The world may forget our seniors, but God does not and wise people also do not. The idea of retirement is basically a new and Western concept, but the truth is that in the kingdom of God there is no such thing as retirement; our roles and responsibilities will surely change as we age, but the fact that we have a responsible role will never change. It is interesting too, that we sometimes think that if we just have enough time we will become mature and we will have attained a certain level of spirituality, however, this is not true. Time is a necessary element of growth, but time, by itself alone, does not bring maturity, which is why we see some men who are well into their seventies, yet still acting very foolishly, they may be old, but they are not a disciple.

Can we look afresh and see that an old disciple is a seasoned warrior of battles, a tempered weapon in the hands of God, an experienced, burden-bearing intercessor, a dignified veteran of church and family life; can we see, indeed, that each one is a priceless and irreplaceable treasure?

Are you the Author?

1 Corinthians 14:46 - What? Came the word of God out from you? Or, came it unto you only?

Human nature has not changed since the beginning of time or, shall we say, at least since the fall of Adam. That is why the Scriptures are continually current. God's word will never be out of date because it simply states things as they are, and its' true principles always correlate to our circumstances and our condition. It has been said that we do not actually read the Bible; it reads us. The word of God cuts through all the facade of our self-confident arrogance and self-imposed ignorance and pierces the heart with truth.

In Paul's letters to the Corinthians we learn much about human nature and certain tendencies which are our collective and continual struggle today, as well. If we read and study closely, and listen with humility, we can gain wisdom and avoid falling into the same traps as they did.

The Corinthians had many problems, but one major recurring nuisance was the issue of pride. Paul, in his distinctive fashion, deals directly with the trouble, like a surgeon with a scalpel, cutting out the cancer, and his words apply very fittingly to us today.

Paul uses questions to shock them and arouse thought; What? He seems surprised and almost appalled. What? How dare any of you to think this way. How audacious. How impudent. You obviously have a short memory, as it was only a few years ago that I came to you bearing the Word of God. Have you forgotten? All parents understand the use of this question. What? What did you do? What did you say? What were you thinking?

How arrogant of us to imagine that the Word of God originated with us, or that we are somehow more special than others, but isn't that exactly what we do when we portray ourselves as the only group that is being used of God to reach people and bring about change in our land? Now, granted, we do not vocalize that terminology because we know that to speak that way would be the peak of self-exaltation, however we certainly do imply these things in the way and the manner which we conduct ourselves. The message is received loud and clear without verbalizing it. We are the ones among whom the revelation has come. We are the ones whom God has entrusted with this message and we have been chosen for His using. We might not say it but, by that attitude we look down our noses at our poor brothers who obviously do not have the light. Apparently, they simply, are not able to receive the truth that we have been entrusted with.

To believe that the Word of God has come out from us only, would be as ridiculous as believing that the alphabet originated with us. No, the alphabet is a gift from God to us and it is the building blocks with which we build. We did not create it and we cannot assume authorship of it. The raw materials are God's, in fact, He is the Alpha and Omega; He is the alphabet. There are no other letters that exist; we don't need any other ones, in fact, it is vain and useless to look for more. He is ultimate completion and we are complete in Him. The only thing that we need to do is to creatively assemble the letters and prayerfully combine the words to bring His Word and His Message to our culture and the people around us.

The Word of God is given to us through many different channels, but it does not originate in the channel; it originates with God. He has chosen to reveal Himself to us through His Word. He has mercifully disclosed His heart to us and, because of that, we can know Him and walk with Him. Instead of being prideful about the portion of truth we have, we should simply be grateful; grateful that God has opened our eyes and allowed us to see Him and to hear His voice. No, the Word of God did not come out from us and it did not come to us only. It is His Word that comes from His heart and it is for all people.

Thank you, Father God for bringing your Word to us; you have radically changed our lives and thank you for allowing us to be channels of your message of grace and healing to others!

Beware of Hypocrisy

Luke 12:1, 2 – Beware of the leaven of the Pharisees, which is hypocrisy. For there is nothing covered, that shall not be revealed, neither hid, that shall not be known.

Jesus gives His disciples a sharp warning to be very cautious and alert regarding the leaven of the Pharisees. Leaven is yeast. It is hidden undetected in the loaf; it penetrates and permeates the dough, thereby thoroughly influencing it. It is hidden; it is unseen, yet it is constantly working. Leaven is like gravity; a silent, unremitting and powerful influence.

The Pharisees were those who separated themselves from common people and things. They were considered by others to be very spiritual and they were highly regarded. Because of this high regard and the sense of being separate and uncommon, the Pharisees developed a sense of superiority and entitlement. They felt that they had special privileges and they were exempt from the laws that governed common people. They were above the law, if you will.

Hypocrisy is the inevitable posture of spiritual pride. Pride, like leaven, is insidious. Arrogant pride is a terrible thing just simply from a natural standpoint; nobody likes arrogance in others. But religious, or spiritual pride, is the highest form of arrogance because it is hidden in actions that appear to be godly and sincere.

Hypocrisy is a word that comes from the theatre. It refers to the actors, who, when wanting to portray a certain character or emotion, would put on a mask. One mask might portray joy, and another might depict sorrow. One mask might represent surprise, and another might illustrate anger. So, hypocrisy is wearing a mask and it has come to stand for ultimate phoniness. If we consistently wear a mask, we have become actors on the stage of life, playing the role of that which we are not. We hide behind the façade of spirituality and godly sincerity.

With insight that could only be divine, Jesus has wonderfully warned all of us. He has told us that there is nothing covered, or hidden behind a mask, or otherwise, that shall not be revealed and known. Is it possible that this leaven of hypocrisy has penetrated our Christianity and influenced our lives today? I believe it has and the threat is ongoing and real. Having simply an outward form of religion forces us to wear a mask; we are not able to be ourselves under that system, or way of thinking. Our current culture many times promotes the wearing of a mask because we really might not want people to truly be themselves. The hardship and the hurts of life can also be a factor in the continued use of masks; I've been betrayed, who can I trust?

What masks are we hiding behind? What are we portraying to the world? Are we wearing a mask of a hard-working, tax-paying citizen, all the while murmuring about the boss and the government? Are we wearing a mask of the committed church member and at the same time very upset with the leadership and people of the church? Are we wearing a mask of the happy-go-lucky person while deeply struggling with fear and sadness? I dare say that all of us wear masks to some degree because part of it is a natural reflex and built-in defence system. One writer once wrote, that the self that we send out to meet God is almost always a false self. Sometimes we may not even be aware that we are doing these things because we have done it for so long it has become second nature. Some of us might hide behind our books, or hard work, or we might throw ourselves into activities that keep us busy; too busy to slow down and get quiet and hear our Father's voice calling us to Himself.

Be encouraged, friends, the first step is to be aware of our tendencies and patterns. Then we must gather to ourselves a couple close friends, or trusted counsellors. Be open, be honest, be free and over time the masks will come off then you, and the rest of the world, will be re-introduced to your true self;

the one created in the image of God; a person of great value and unique talents; one who has a beautiful and bright future.

Section Five

Relationships

> *The way in which two or more people are connected.*
>
> *Oxford Dictionary*

The Greatest Thing in the World

1 Corinthians 13:4 - Love suffers long and is kind.

Isn't it fascinating that the very first thing Paul says about love is that it will suffer? It will undergo and experience some form of pain, hurt or hardship. It almost seems as if love must suffer and it must undergo testing, for it to be proven to be real love. Love cares and feels deeply; hence it has the potential to suffer. If I do not love someone or care for them, then their hurtful actions towards me, or their negligence of me, could not cause me to suffer. Genuine love is completely exposed and vulnerable. It removes any defenses and drops its guard, thus exposing itself to the possibilities of being hurt and suffering pain and damage.

C. S. Lewis writes something very pertinent

regarding this; "...There is no safe investment. To love at all is to be vulnerable. Love anything and your heart will be wrung and possibly broken. If you want to make sure of keeping it intact you must give it to no one, not even an animal. Wrap it carefully round with hobbies and little luxuries; avoid all entanglements. Lock it up safe in the casket or coffin of your selfishness. But in that casket, safe, dark, motionless, airless, it will change. It will not be broken; it will become unbreakable, impenetrable, irredeemable...."

There is something about love that allows itself to suffer; it never defends itself, but takes each blow as it faithfully absorbs the pain. Paul says earlier to the Corinthians, 'Why do you not rather take wrong? why do you not rather suffer yourselves to be defrauded?' I believe it is important, because many people live in abusive and boundary-less relationships, that we are clear about what it means to walk in love. While we know that love is so strong that it can stand any kind of treatment, that doesn't mean that one is supposed to stay in an abusive relationship.

Every person needs to allow the Holy Spirit to guide them; there is different guidance from God for different situations.

Love suffers, but not just a momentary, fleeting suffering, but it suffers for a long time. It is never tired of waiting, it is never in a hurry, and it will continue to undergo suffering however long is necessary. The reason that love suffers long is that, by nature, it is committed and therefore the thought of quitting on that relationship cannot be considered. Time is irrelevant to love. It is a spiritual strength that causes one to rise above the daily grind of time.

The two words suffer and long, are one compound word in the original text; macrothumia is the word in the Greek and it is translated longsuffering. We use the word 'macro' to describe the big picture. It is a word of perspective. We sometimes say, 'He can't see the forest for the trees', in other words, he is too close to the situation to see it in perspective. He has a micro view and needs to step back and look at it from a distance. That is the word 'macro', it means 'from a distance'. Love has a macro view, it sees the big picture, and it suffers long. When your teenager is struggling with various temptations normal to those years, you, as a parent, have a bigger picture and so, therefore, you can calmly deal with it.

The word 'thumia' is the word for temper or anger. The opposite of long-tempered is short-tempered and we know how quickly that gets us in trouble. Love is not short-tempered; it doesn't easily blow a fuse, we might say. Being short-tempered demonstrates that we do not have a big picture and proper perspective of what we are facing. If we respond to our circumstance too quickly, we can make matters worse.

Proverbs tells us, 'He that is slow to wrath is of great understanding: but he that is hasty of spirit exalts folly.' Expressing love comes easier to those who have developed the skill of understanding another person. Stephen Covey has taught us to 'seek first to understand, then to be understood.' The macro view enables us to have perspective which, in turn gives us an understanding of the person or situation we are having conflict with. If we can truly understand how that person could do what they did, then compassion can flow unhindered. I understand how that could happen. Given all the same circumstances and pressures, over time, any one of us could have done that very same thing or worse.

Perspective and understanding are linked. Perspective shows how things are connected and how they stand in relation to another. Once you get that bigger picture, understanding occurs. Then understanding engenders sympathy and sympathy releases compassion, and isn't that the greatest thing in the world?

Forgiveness is a Bridge

Luke 23:34 - Then said Jesus, Father, forgive them; for they know not what they do.

This is one of the precious Seven Words from the Cross, spoken by Jesus under intense suffering. There is a vast body of literature that has been written and preached, over the centuries, on these sayings and oh, how rich the literature is. Some have said that Jesus still had things that He must say before He died, so He preached them from the most sacred of all pulpits; the pulpit of the Cross.

Even while He is undergoing the worst type of torture and pain known to man, Jesus is thinking of others. Love is ever thinking of others; never of itself. Truly, Jesus' life portrayed the ultimate selfless Man. Save yourself, one of the thieves said, but it could never be, He didn't come to save Himself; He came to save others. He came to save us, to save you, and to save me.

He is still looking to His Father; the source of love and forgiveness. Father forgive them. That is why you sent me, to forgive; to see mankind released from their sin. Forgiveness is the bridge between the Father and 'them', please build that bridge, Father. Release the prisoners and unlock the shackles that have bound them. It has been said that forgiveness is like setting the prisoner free, and then, realizing that the prisoner was you. Father, release them, free them, liberate them, and let them cross that bridge. All forgiveness ultimately comes from the Father. We would not truly know forgiveness if it weren't for Him. The Father is the one who created us, and He is the one who remains committed to us regardless of our stance toward Him.

Do not hold this against them; they do not understand what they are doing. Most people are crowd influenced and driven. Most of the people in this crowd were simply caught up in the frenzy and emotions of the moment; they did not understand what was really happening behind the scenes, so to speak. Paul tells us that 'if the princes of this world had known, they would not have crucified the Lord of Glory'. The Jewish leaders did not know. Pilate and Herod did not know. The crowd did not know, and the soldiers did not know. None of them truly knew the significance of this event. God, however, knew exactly what was happening and he knew that for forgiveness to become available to all, there must be a sacrifice. Jesus was the Lamb of God who would bear away the sin of the world by accepting the weight of other people's rebellious choices.

That's what forgiveness does; it doesn't do away with the wrong done, but it releases people from their self-imposed chains. Unforgiveness burns the bridge over which we, ourselves, may one day need to cross. Let's not be bridge burners, but instead, be bridge builders. Father, we look to you for the love and the grace to follow the example of Jesus and continue to forgive ourselves and others.

Is There Ever Friendly Fire?

2 Corinthians 2:11 - Lest Satan should get an advantage of us: for we are not ignorant of his devices.

We are in a war and this war has a very real enemy. Even the word satan means adversary, or opponent. It is so easy to walk through this life forgetting that there is an invisible battle going on all around us. One preacher has encouraged us to remember that this world more of a battleground than a playground. The reality is that we are in a fight, and this fight has actual casualties.

Satan, our enemy, seeks an advantage over us. Isn't that what armies do? They seek the most strategic places and try to get the high ground, or the best vantage point, where an all-out assault can be made. We cannot be ignorant of how our enemy works. He has methods of operation and tactics of warfare which we must be informed of. Paul says do not be unaware of his devices.

In these recent days, when Canadian soldiers have been stationed in various Middle Eastern places, we hear a lot about IEDs, which are Improvised Explosive Devices. These devices are usually hidden, and the unsuspecting and unaware soldier can unknowingly trigger the explosion. We must not be ignorant, uninformed or unaware of this tactic of the enemy.

The context of Paul's writing speaks of unforgiveness. We must forgive, or our opponent will gain the advantage and overpower us. Talk about an explosive device; the longer unforgiveness sits hidden and invisible, the more serious the damage can be. If we are not both diligent and vigilant, we can easily allow bitter feelings to enter and linger in our hearts. The fact is, while our warfare is with satan, we almost always battle with each other. If we can be divided and distracted from the actual fight, or if we unwittingly turn our weapons on each other, then our foe has already done his work. Be alert! Be aware! Be awake! We have a malicious and dangerous opponent whose one aim is to kill and destroy anything that resembles God and reminds him of what he has lost and what he will never regain. We are hated and hunted. Let's not do the hating and hunting on behalf of our enemy; there's certainly nothing friendly about that fire.

Watch Your Mouth

Galatians 5:15 - But if you bite and devour one another, take heed that you be not consumed one of another.

Biting and devouring is done with the mouth. The mouth is an unusually important part of the body. We eat our food through our mouth and we also speak words through our mouth. We are told in the book of Proverbs that death and life is in the power of the tongue. We can either speak life or death; it is our choice. We can speak blessing or cursing by our own decision. Paul says if you continue to bite and devour one another you will eventually consume each other.

Negative words eat as a slow working acid; they are corrosive, pervasive and destructive. What kind of power have we been given that we can actually destroy each other with our words? What kind of words am I speaking, not

only to another, but about another? Quite
often we are pleasant and civil to each other's
face, but then we get behind closed doors and
we say things that are not from a motive of
love. Love desires the best for the other
person. Do we truly love one another? If we
allowed love to govern us, we simply would
not be able to speak any other type of words,
but words of love and grace and blessing.
Even words of correction must come from a
heart of love. It does not mean that we will
see everything eye to eye, but we can easily
disagree without being disagreeable.

Scripture exhorts us to have a deep
affection for one another. Do I have a deep
affection for the family of God? Affection is
warm and sincere; it is not phony. While we all
have different personalities, I believe that love
transcends all personality types and compels
all of us to show genuine love and affection.
Jesus said that the world would know that we
are his disciples because of the love we have
for each other and the way we treat each
other. Does the way I relate to my brothers
and sisters in Christ demonstrate to others

that I am a believer? Is there something different about the way I behave toward the family of God?

The world is not a very kind place; it can be quite the opposite. The Christian world, however, can and must be, a place where all people are accepted, and all are valued. Many things in life are not in our control, but we can control the words that we speak. We can determine to speak words motivated by love and be bodybuilders, not destroyers.

Your Answer is in Others

Acts 10:5, 6 - And now send men to Joppa, and call for one Simon, whose surname is Peter: He lodges with one Simon a tanner, whose house is by the sea side: he shall tell you what you ought to do.

Imagine standing in the very presence of an angel of God, hearing him speak and seeing him a just a few feet away from you. This is what Cornelius experienced. It was, apparently, during a time of prayer that the angel appeared to him. An angel came directly to him; an actual messenger from God was dispatched from heaven to speak to Cornelius. What amazing truth would he reveal? What powerful insights and divine privileges would he share? What celestial mysteries would Cornelius be invited into?

The angel informs Cornelius that his prayer has been heard. How this must have caused his heart to swell with anticipation and expectation of good. 'My prayer has been heard. God Almighty has heard my prayer. I have had a hearing in the presence of the Highest.' Cornelius is described to us as a man who prayed to God always. Today we would describe the same type of man as a man of prayer. Prayer is relationship with God not just asking him for things. Prayer includes worship and adoration, and, also, specific requests and petitions. No doubt Cornelius included both in his lifestyle of prayer.

'Your prayer has been heard.' There is a strong implication that God does not necessarily hear every prayer. However, if God has heard our prayer, then he has also provided an answer to it. If we know that he hears us, then we know that we have been granted the petition that we have asked of him. I believe that the deepest desire and prayer of Cornelius' heart was that he would know God fully and, that he would be able to lead his family into a more intimate relationship with God. He was a man that feared and reverenced God above the average person. So, when the angel said that his prayer had been heard, he would have expected that the next words out of the angel's mouth would reveal his answer.

'Call for one Simon, whose surname is Peter,' These instructions from the angel might seem, to some people, to be a bit of a letdown. An angel with a message from God himself tells Cornelius that he must meet someone and that person would tell him what he needed to hear. Why didn't the angel simply tell him directly? Surely the angel knew what Cornelius needed, however, God has designed his plan to include people. He loves to work through us as we yield and obey his instructions. It is the will of God for us to have God-ordained relationships and connections with others. Cornelius must meet Peter. Peter must also meet Cornelius. God is at work in both men's lives simultaneously, and he uses this powerful meeting to reveal another important aspect of his divine strategy. Not only does Cornelius and his family come into a more complete salvation, but Peter also is undeniably shown that God desires all men of every nation to come into personal relationship and salvation.

Do not be surprised that when your prayer has been heard, that the answer will come by meeting the right people. We cannot fulfill the will of God without others in our life. If we could fulfill the will and plan of God by ourselves, how come we haven't? This is one of the reasons that I believe so strongly in the power of the local church and being connected to people who know us. I pray that we would have the humility to receive the answer from God through whomever he chooses to use. Get ready for your answer, but, just remember, that it may come in the form of an ordinary and familiar man named Peter.

Peter's Commission

Luke 22:32 – "...strengthen your brothers..."

The commands of God are not complicated, they are simple, and, in their simplicity, they are deeply profound. Peter is not given a long and convoluted set of instructions, but he is merely given three words from Jesus that He followed for the rest of his life. We also are to follow these words and make them a life-long practice; we are to strengthen our brothers.

We are not called to criticize, or complain about our brothers, nor to demean them; we are called to strengthen them. Strength answers many problems and challenges in life. If we are strong, we can go through difficult seasons courageously and not be overcome by them. A trial of sickness can be endured if we have strength. Financial difficulty and pressures can be bravely faced if we have strength. Relationship trouble, betrayal, divorce, and even, the loss of a loved one, cannot defeat us, if we have strength. Paul confirms this fact when he said that he could do all things through Christ who strengthened him.

For Peter, the brothers may have represented three categories. First, they were his Hebrew brothers; he was called to strengthen their faith in the One True God. Secondly, they were his brothers in Christ; he was called to strengthen their faith in the Lord Jesus Christ and in His plan for their lives. Thirdly, they were his brothers of humanity; he was called to strengthen their faith as good citizens and builders of a healthy home and family life.

They are my brothers and I have an innate responsibility to add strength to their life. As members of a family we understand first-hand that the brothers will inevitably have conflict. The very first family reveals the tendency for sibling rivalry and relationship trouble; indeed, Cain did not fulfill his role as his brother's keeper.

Notice in this instance that Peter is not told to go evangelize and bring in new people; he is told to strengthen the existing people. We do, indeed, have a Great Commission to reach the world with the Gospel message, but what are we bringing people into? If we do not strengthen our home base there is nothing for others to re-build their lives upon.

Each of us has daily opportunities to strengthen others. We mustn't take anything away from people, but always give something to them. Find something in their life that you can support and strengthen. Leave them better off after you have spoken to them. Help, assist, contribute, build and reinforce. What would our homes be like if we constantly strengthened all those within it? How about our workplace, or our church? Let's be those who are known for their positive contribution; let's be part of the solution, not part of the problem. Strengthen those around you, encourage those around you, look for a way to be constructive; strengthen the brothers!

That's a Bitter Pill to Swallow

Hebrews 12:15 - Looking diligently lest any man fail of the grace of God; lest any root of bitterness springing up trouble you, and thereby many be defiled.

Scripture is chockfull with warnings that caution us, and exhortations that remind us, that we play a vital role in our own safety and health. We cannot assume that negative things will never happen to us. All are susceptible to becoming hurt, offended and ending up being bitter; no one is completely sheltered from that threat. Diligence is required; we need unusual thoroughness. Vigilance is necessary; we need unusual attentiveness. Look diligently, look consistently, be aware, be alert and be awake; danger lurks around every corner. If there were no real risk, there would be no clear warning to beware.

There are none who are exempt from the human tendency to step outside of the grace of God. It is important to realize that there are always two sides to everything; there is God's side and man's side. On God's side, He is always faithful, and because of that, the grace of God could never fail, but on our side, we can fail and walk away from the blessing and protection of God's grace. One man has written that every step out of love is a step into sin, and by that definition, all of us have sinned and stepped out from under the umbrella of grace.

Bitterness does not come in seed form; it usually shows up much later as a deeply rooted plant that has sprung up from unassuming and inconspicuous seed. Those seeds might come in the shape of hurt feelings or thoughts of mistreatment, and because they come in a small form it is easy to ignore their presence and not deal with them immediately. However, if we are wise, then we will be watching diligently and guarding over the thought-seeds that come our way, and by so doing, we will keep ourselves in the love of

God and we will never have the trouble that comes with a root of bitterness.

Bitterness has a way of spreading contagiously. Like a bad weed in your garden, it grows at a rapid pace without any effort of your own. Let's be careful to guard our hearts and protect them from the poison of bitterness, for many are the people who did not intend on allowing themselves to become bitter and hard-hearted. All of us can fall prey if we are not always aware. If we keep ourselves full of the love of God, He will protect us and we will be able to finish our race of life with energy to spare.

Section Six

Growth

" *A stage in the process of growing, progressive development.*

Merriam-Webster

We are the Channel, not the Source

Acts 3:4 - And Peter, fastening his eyes upon him with John, said, Look on us.

Acts 3:12 - And when Peter saw it, he answered unto the people, You men of Israel, why marvel at this? or why look so earnestly on us, as though by our own power or holiness we had made this man to walk?

Peter and John were on their way to the temple to pray when they came across this lame man who had been brought there daily by others for many years. He was placed there at the gate to the temple in hope that some kind person would have mercy on him and give him enough money to squeak by and survive another day.

This account reminds us that there are always those suffering souls around us that cry out to be seen. I once asked my son, Wesley, who was in his mid-twenties at the time, what the greatest need of his generation was. His answer was profound and given unhesitatingly; they need to be noticed. Isn't that what we all need? How piercing these words are to those of us who march quickly through our daily activities and tasks, but do not have eyes to see the people who are placed in our path. Peter, however, not only saw the man, but took a deep interest in him and his plight; indeed, we are told that he fastened his eyes on him. The lame man was unaware of who he was encountering, nor what he was about to receive. He thought he was going to get some loose change, and, in fact, he had his chains loosed. But let's look closer at Peter's instruction to the man.

Look on us. Notice that it is not, 'Look on me'. Peter does not elevate himself above John, and John, likewise, does not grasp for attention; they are content to work together. This is a powerful thought when we realize that Peter and John had some previous relationship struggle and conflict. They had different personalities and views, but God did a deep work in their hearts that caused them to be united from then on. We are brothers and sisters in the Lord; we are members of the same body of Christ; we have the same mission, and that mission is about people. It is encouraging to see these men of God cooperate, both with God and each other. Someone once said that it is amazing what can be accomplished if we do not care who gets the credit.

This dear man was born lame and would never have known a normal care-free childhood. He would not have had the blessing of productive work or having a mate in life. He was unable to go anywhere without assistance; he was what we might call today, the marginalized of society; sidelined and disregarded. He could not stand up and walk as God created him to, and maybe one of the most tragic things was he couldn't look people in the eyes as their peer. He was lowered by the harsh realities of his life, indeed, everyone looked down on him. But one day he heard someone tell him to look up, look out and to look at who it was that was speaking to him. Our answers lie not in lifeless money but, in a living person.

Look on us. We are here to help. We are sent by God. We do not have all the answers, but we know the One who does. We are not the Source of your answer, but we may very well be the channel. We are the conduit for the Power to flow through. Look on us, for you may not be able to see God, but you can see us. You may not be hearing His voice, but you can hear ours.

After the man was healed there was quite a commotion among the people because they all knew the man and had observed him begging daily at the gate of the temple. No doubt, many people began to credit the amazing miracle to Peter and John and point toward them as Healers and Miracle-Workers. Many men, whom God has used, have gone astray just here. Had these men not walked closely with Jesus, and saw His humility and how He credited the Father for all the great things that took place through His ministry, they might have been tempted to receive some of that praise, but these godly and sensible men wanted nothing to do with that.

Why are you looking on us? We are men just like you. We are no different, and certainly not better. We do not have any power of our own and we are not any more holy than others. We wanted the lame man to look on us because he needed the answer, but now that he has his answer, we want you to look to God as the Source of this great miracle. I fastened my eyes on him when he was in need, but you must not fasten your eyes on us now that the need is met. Jesus must get all the credit. He is the reason that this man is healed. He is the one to be praised.

Our lives are made up of many different seasons and circumstances. One day we might be in Peter and John's position, being used by God as a channel of blessing. Another day we might be in the lame man's position, needing

God's blessing. More accurately, I suppose, we are simultaneously in both positions. We are the needy being used of God to meet needs. We are the helpless being used of God to bring help. We are the weak being used of God to bring strength. We are the sick, being used of God to bring healing. We are the sorrowful being used of God to bring joy. We are the momentary being used of God to bring the eternal. It is wonderful to be a channel through whom God can flow, but one thing we know for sure; we are merely the channel and not the Source. All the credit, all the praise and all the honour must go to whom it is rightly due; our precious Saviour and Lord, Jesus the Christ!

God is Able

Ephesians 3:20, 21 - Now unto him that is able to do exceeding abundantly above all that we ask or think, according to the power that works in us, Unto him be glory in the church by Christ Jesus throughout all ages, world without end. Amen.

God is able. Those three words have infused faith and courage in the hearts of believers for two thousand years, and they continue to do so today. God is able. He is the Supreme and Almighty God and he is also our Father who is with us and for us. God is able. I am reminded of something that James S. Stewart wrote in one of his excellent writings, 'The constant watchword of the New Testament is not "We are able", but what you do find over and over again is, "He is able", and when they say it, they are looking away from themselves to God.' God is the one who has all ability, capability, power and might. He is able. These words evoke a reverent and worshipful response from within us.

We could dwell on the ability of God and admire and worship him forever, however, this verse tells us that God is not just able, but that he is able to do something. God has ability that he desires to use; he wants his ability to be put into action and to produce a result. What is it that he is able to do? He is able to exceed abundantly above all that we ask or think. That is an amazing statement. One expanded version even says that he is able to do 'infinitely beyond our highest prayers, desires, thoughts, hopes, or dreams.' Just consider what you could ask God for, and then consider also what you could imagine God doing, then multiply that by the words; exceeding abundantly above. Is that ten times higher? Is that one hundred times higher? Is it a thousand times higher? No! It is infinitely higher. In other words, there is no limit to what God's ability can do. God is able.

But, let's keep reading. God is able to do

this according to the power that is working in us. God is able but he planned for that ability to work in accordance, and in cooperation, with us. He wants to use us as his vessels; his channels of power and blessing to others. God has given us a powerful privilege and an amazing responsibility called choice. Our ability to choose by an act of our will is one of the things that sets us apart from the rest of creation and places us in the 'image of God' category. Animals have choice, but, for the most part, they are driven by instinct and survival. We certainly are not able to choose everything that happens to us, but we definitely can choose our response. A survivor of the Nazi concentration camps, Victor Frankl, once wrote that 'Everything can be taken from a man but one thing: the last of the human freedoms—to choose one's attitude in any given set of circumstances, to choose one's own way.'

Is God's power at work in us? Has that power become inactive and static, lying dormant within? The fact of the matter is that we must constantly stir up the power within us, we must hunger for that power to be reactivated in us and released through us. God's will is to do amazing and powerful things through each one of our lives. He wants to. He desires to. He longs to. However, He will not force or override our will; he desires our willingness and cooperation in the execution of His will. One time a friend of mine was having marriage problems to the point where his wife's heart had grown cold towards him; she didn't love him anymore. I said to him, 'You don't want your wife to love you.' His response was, 'I don't?' I said, 'No, what you want is for your wife to want to love you.' God is looking for those who want to. He wants to pour out His Spirit through those vessels who want Him to. God's infinite ability is released according to the power that is active in you and I.

Words are Containers and Conveyors

Acts 11:14 - Who shall tell you words, whereby you and all your house shall be saved.

The angel that appeared to Cornelius told him to send for Peter, who, when he came, would speak the very words needed to experience salvation. A friend of mine used to say that the answer is not a 'what', but a 'who'. In other words, we look for answers in things, and God looks for answers in people. We attempt many times to develop a new program or system, and systems are indeed necessary, but unless we have the right people in those systems, they will not be productive. The right people must be in the right place, at the right time, doing the right thing. Both Peter and Cornelius certainly fall into this category. I love the way that God supernaturally choreographs this whole scenario. In one city, Cornelius is being prepared by God, through an angelic visitation, to send for Peter and, simultaneously, in another city, Peter is being prepared by God, through a vision, to be sent to Cornelius. Like a master chef preparing all the ingredients for a nutritious meal, God arranges all the elements for an impactful meeting.

The angel instructs Cornelius to send for Peter, and he also piques his interest by saying that Peter will tell him certain words, and those words will contain a message and instructions that will result in salvation for him and his household. We can imagine the expectation that must have arose within Cornelius' heart, as he gathered his family and friends together and waited for Peter to come. We can envision this leader speaking to those gathered. 'I have had a very unusual experience. I have had an angel visit me and give me specific directions to obey. We are obviously being invited into something very important. Let us prepare our hearts for what we will hear. We are going to hear words; words that will convey a powerful message from God. We have been praying about our place in God's plan and we know that there is something missing. We are serving God and living right but there is still a void within our hearts. These words which we are about to hear will answer our heart cry.' I believe that one of the reasons for the great outpouring of the Spirit that took place, after Peter arrived, was the anticipation in the hearts of Cornelius and his friends; there is no doubt that God is attracted to the hungry heart.

God uses men as his vessels; he fills them with his spirit and power; he pours himself out through them. Men, also, use their words as vessels. Words are containers; they contain whatever we place in them. We can fill our words with hate or with love; we can fill them with doubt or with faith. Peter's words, that day, contained the truth centered on Jesus Christ. He spoke the word of God to them and we know that faith comes by hearing the word of God. So, faith was transported into their hearts by the words that Peter spoke, and they received. The words were the vehicle that contained the elements needed for Cornelius and his household to be saved. We must never underestimate the power of our words. Every word that comes out of our mouths has a profound effect both, on ourselves, and others. The gospel of Jesus Christ has been committed to us and we literally have the power to set people free by the spoken word. Words are vessels for carrying spiritual substance; they can contain hatred or love; they can contain frustration or peace; they can contain doubt or faith. What are we carrying in our words?

Three Vital Factors

Acts 24:25 - And as he reasoned of righteousness, temperance, and judgment to come, Felix trembled, and answered, Go your way for this time; when I have a convenient season, I will call for you.

Paul was a master conversationalist. God gave him an ability to speak to men in a way that kept their interest. Jesus had said to Paul that he would stand before the Gentiles and kings. This verse says that he reasoned with Felix concerning three vital spiritual realities; righteousness, temperance and judgement to come.

Righteousness is an often-misunderstood subject. What is it? I have heard several definitions such as; an ability to stand in the presence of God without any sense of condemnation; right standing with God; right living and right ways. The same underlying word is used to describe someone who is just. Righteousness and justice then are related. God is designated in Scripture as the justifier of the ungodly. Whatever our definition, one thing is for sure; we do not make ourselves righteous; we cannot justify ourselves. We need God to make us righteous, and we need him to make us just. That is not in our nature; we must have a new nature from God; a righteous nature. Right standing with God results in being able to be yourself before the Lord. It is the sense of being completely accepted, and therefore, not needing to be false in any way. We can present our true selves to the Lord because that is what he sees anyway, righteousness simply enables us to do so without fear of reprisal. We have been made right through the work of Jesus on the cross; the shedding of his blood. The scripture even speaks about receiving the gift of righteousness; so, if it is indeed a gift, then righteousness can never be earned, it simply must be received and walked in.

Temperance is an old English word which we do not really use much today, however, it is packed full of meaning that certainly applies to us. To temper steel is to make it pliable and flexible, yet stronger and less susceptible to shattering. In the light of that, you would have to agree that we could definitely use some tempering. How many of us have been damaged simply because we have not been able to roll with the punches, so to speak? Many people who have been hurt in car wrecks are hurt because they tried to brace themselves for the impact and the jolt of it damaged their bodies. I have been told that people who are under the influence of alcohol and who end up in a car accident are less likely to be hurt because they are relaxed and flexible. To be tempered by God is to become like a shock absorber, continually adjusting oneself to the contours of the road. Somebody has once said, 'Blessed are the flexible, for they shall not be broken.' One of the things that is evident in life is the need to be tempered by God; to go through a process that causes us to have an adjustable demeanor, adapting ourselves to different circumstances and to varied people. I am definitely not suggesting that we let go of our principles, but that we adjust our practices. My pastor used to tell us that when we faced difficult things it was important to respond and not react; response has the tempered feel to it; reaction seems much more rigid and tense.

The word judgement carries with it mostly negative connotations; a critical, nit-picky boss who loves to point out all your flaws; an angry, heavy-handed man with a gavel in his hand eagerly passing out a sentence of punishment; or maybe, a mean-spirited church-goer who looks down his nose at everyone. However, from God's perspective, judgement is always a positive thing. Everybody wants to be rewarded but there is no reward without judgement. Any contest or competition has a panel of judges who determine whether you win or lose, and even our schools have a system of judgement through examination and grading; no promotion without passing a test. We raise our children with a view to helping them learn to exercise good judgement and wisely choose the proper path in life. Judges preside over court rooms, listening intently as each lawyer argues their case, after which the judgement must be made. Judgement is normal to God's kingdom; he is a judge and he will adjudicate his will in the Earth. According to the New Testament writings, there will be a judgement to come; there will be an account given for how we have lived our lives, and how we have stewarded our skills, our time, and our resources.

Be encouraged, friends, because of the Blood of Jesus and His amazing grace, we can continue to walk in the gift of righteousness, remain yielded to God's process of temperance and stand confidently in the light of his merciful judgement.

Do You Need a Lift?

Matthew 8:15 – And He touched her hand and the fever left her: and she arose, and ministered unto them.

Jesus had just come into Peter's house and, when he did, he saw Peter's mother-in-law lying down with a fever. Doctor Luke in his description says she was 'taken' with a great fever, which in the original language pictures one who was held down and constrained under the power of a life-threatening fever. She was so debilitated by it that she was completely out of commission but Jesus, as always, was immediately aware of her condition. There are several different things occurring here that are worthy of our attention and consideration.

He touched her. Touch implies connection, closeness, and tenderness. Isn't this what everyone needs? We all so desperately need the touch of Jesus. He is always ready and ever reaching out to touch humanity. There is no one outside the scope of His touch; there is no one too sinful or too damaged. The touch of Jesus heals the sufferer; the touch of Jesus cleanses away all sin; the touch of Jesus restores dignity and destiny. He touched her.

He touched her hand. His hand made contact with her hand. He didn't grab her roughly and lift her up; he didn't lay hands on her fevered brow; no, he simply touched her hand. This seems to suggest a calmness; a respect; a dignity with which Jesus ministered; he had dignity, and he preserved her dignity, by not creating great fanfare. Her hand was what brought her joy. It was her hand that gave her the ability to serve in a practical way to others, and she had used her hands all of her life to bless and nurture her family; she had found her niche in life by extending her hand to those around her. He touched her hand.

The fever left her. It almost seems to imply that the fever had personality; it knew that it must respond. The fever was aware that a greater power had arrived and, just as when light enters the room, darkness must flee. The touch of Jesus always causes the enemy to leave. The touch of Jesus always triumphs over every work of the adversary. When the fever left, health came flooding back in; the hindrance to health and strength was dealt with. The fever left her.

She arose. She didn't stay in bed. She didn't say, 'I must rest and recuperate.' She didn't even look for any sympathy. She had no reason, now, to be in bed. 'The fever that held me down is gone so I will arise.' She arose by an act of her will. Moments before she was under the power of the fever; completely incapacitated; without options; and now she has a choice and she used her choice to arise and be a part of the household and a contributor to the community. She arose.

She ministered unto them. What a beautiful picture of a grateful lady. I'm sure that this desire to serve was not new to her; she had always served. Like many of the women we know, she worked hard in so many ways; cleaning, cooking, helping, serving, always putting others ahead of herself. That is why it is significant that Jesus touched her hand. That was part of her gifting and her place of joy and service; to use her hands. She did not use her restored health for self-serving purposes. She didn't go to the mall, so to speak. No! She used her renewed strength to serve in menial ways to others. She put others needs ahead of her own. She ministered unto them.

Peter's mother-in-law was one of those who ministered anonymously and silently; behind the scenes. She may remain nameless to us, but there is no doubt that she was not nameless to those of her family and those within her circle of friends. They knew her name and they knew her reputation; they saw her self-less service and they benefited from her ministering hands. Heaven also knows her name for no service ever goes unseen by our God in Heaven. He sees the servant's heart. These are the ones whom the Lord Jesus uses as vessels of His ministering heart. His heart reaches and touches humanity through our hands; what a privilege; what a joy; what a life!

These Boots Were Made for Walking

Genesis 5:24 - And Enoch walked with God: and he was not; for God took him.

What a privilege to be invited to walk with God. Walking is natural and normal to life, so we are being encouraged to take our natural, normal life and use it to walk with God. Take your life and align it with His; Enoch with God; the natural with the spiritual; the common with the uncommon; the human with the divine. When there was no mention of any of his peers walking with God, Enoch chose a path and a direction in life by choosing to walk with God.

We are not born with the ability to walk; the potential for it is there, but we must develop and grow into that skill. Our muscles must develop, and our balance must improve, before we can begin. To walk implies that we have started on a path of growth. It is a great day in the home, when the little child takes its first steps; everyone gets excited. We can only imagine how God must also get excited when His little ones develop to the point where they are not being carried, but are choosing to walk and carry their own weight.

Man is created to walk upright; we do not crawl forever. In fact, if your child does not start walking by a certain age, there is great reason to be concerned; something is wrong. Walking brings with it new-found freedom for the child, and, simultaneously, it brings a lot less freedom for the parents. The child has become much more active, mobile and able to choose directions and locations. Even though it is more difficult for us as parents, we want our children to mature and begin making some of their own decisions; it is our will for them. They are designed to stand up, and to stand tall, and to make choices.

Enoch chose to walk, but he didn't walk alone; he wanted to accompany someone, and he wanted the company of another; he decided to walk with God. To be with someone implies relationship, friendship and partnership. Being with someone also necessitates a proximity; we cannot walk with another if there is distance between us. Unlike many today, Enoch did not desire to be a loner; he did not isolate himself; he chose companionship; he chose someone to walk through life with. Who you choose to walk with is vitally important, and Enoch revealed his inner character by choosing God.

The fact that we can walk with God says a lot about God's heart. If I have a young child and the child wants to walk with me, I will have to adjust for that to happen. I will have to lower myself, come to the child's level and slow down my pace. No good father will think it is a burden to have to do this; it is a joy to walk with your child.

The book of Amos asks us, 'How can two walk together unless they are in agreement?' There must be agreement about the time and place to meet for a walk. There must be agreement about the direction and the speed with which you will walk. There must be agreement about the purpose of the walk. Quite often, my wife will suggest that we go for a walk, but most always, we have two different things in mind. I'm thinking about going for a leisurely stroll and she is thinking about a vigorous exercise. I'm thinking of flat ground and she has a hill in mind; indeed, there must be agreement. In our walk with God there will also be times that may require a different pace or a different purpose.

To walk with God implies that we have taken some time with Him and have gone a fair distance, not just a few steps. Enoch walked with God through all the seasons of life; he enjoyed the good times and he endured the bad times; he continued to walk through the triumphs and through the trials; through the joys and the sorrows. He kept pace with God and no matter which way life was pulling him, he walked in God's direction. He spent his life walking with God, not noticing that he was changing as they walked.

There is a phrase spoken by John the

Baptist that seems to resemble what happened to Enoch; 'He must increase, but I must decrease.' He must become more prominent, and I must become less prominent. He must become more visible, and I must become less visible. His wisdom must be forefront, and my wisdom must be secondary. Things were becoming less about Enoch and more about God, and it seemed to happen almost effortlessly. It took place over time as he kept walking with God. Many times, we might struggle to overcome certain habits or resist certain temptations; indeed, we all have character flaws and we all have much room for growth. However, if we focus only on those things that we need to change it can sometimes make it harder. Enoch walked with God and his personal problems took care of themselves; he walked with God and was not.

Someone has once said that Enoch and God had walked together for so long that they got closer to God's house than they were to Enoch's, so God just took him to His home. Be encouraged friends, God desires to walk with us; it is His idea; and He has made us able to walk with Him. We might stumble here and there on the journey, but we must keep walking and keep in step with God and soon, very soon, we will see that we have arrived at the door to His house. The peace, joy and pleasures which await us there are far beyond anything that any of us could even begin to imagine! Thank you, Jesus!

The Human Tendency to Err

Mark 12:24 – Do you not therefore err, because you know not the Scriptures neither the power of God?

The Sadducees were very well-versed in the Old Testament writings and, yet, Jesus said that they did not know the Scriptures. Apparently, it is possible to read, memorize and recite verses and, yet, still not know them. This thought should alarm us and cause us to take a little closer look at our own Bible knowledge, and by so doing, this thought will also arm us.

The condition of mankind is such that we think we know something when we actually know so very little and even the small part that we do know, we may not know very well. There are two kinds of knowledge. There is one that says, 'I know that because I have read it, or heard it', and the other that says, 'I know that because I practice it.' In our modern Western culture, we are immersed in so-called knowledge, we are saturated in it, and yet, we do not seem to be any better off. These Sadducees were saturated in the Scriptures, they had memorized it and could quote large sections, but Jesus informs them that they did not know the Scriptures. The ancient Eastern view of knowledge is described by the words, 'Adam knew his wife and she conceived.' This kind of knowledge is relational knowledge; it is knowledge within the context of a relationship. We do not know someone because we simply know a lot of facts about them, we only truly know someone by regular communication, interaction and conversation. This is a living and active knowledge; not head-knowledge, but heart knowledge; not book-knowledge, but biological knowledge; not organized, but organic. If we do not come into this vital knowledge, we will continue to err.

To err is to be deceived; it means to wander or roam from a place of safety, truth or virtue. This is the human problem; we stray, we wander, we are easily seduced. Deception is the enemy's greatest weapon and sadly, we have unleashed it upon ourselves. As a society, we have been infected with deception and the poison of it is spreading rapidly. There is now almost nothing that is not believable or acceptable to us. We have, indeed, roamed far from home.

Unfortunately, the same is true for many churches and Christians. We have neglected the Scripture and pursued our own ideas of truth and how our lives should be lived. Jesus said that the cause of our deception and roaming was our lack of truly knowing the Scriptures, and because of that, we have not accessed the power of God. If we do not come back to Scriptural education and Biblical preaching, the kind that accesses power and produces a living relationship with God, we will continue to gain speed in our slide down the slope of error.

I once read a powerful little story by Jack London called, 'To Build a Fire.' It was about a man that had gone out into the wilderness in extremely cold weather and ended up being overcome by it and dying. In this short story London makes a statement about the man; 'He was quick and alert in the things of life, but only in the things, not in their significance.' The man understood the facts about the extreme cold, but he didn't catch its' real significance and meaning. He didn't consider what that meant for him as a frail and delicate human. That phrase seems to fit here, and we could be like that man. We could be quick and alert regarding the facts of Scripture; understand the context and quote verses verbatim, but miss the true meaning and how it applies to our daily life. The power of Scripture is released only when we understand the meaning of it; its real significance.

I want to encourage you, friends, to take time to slow down and smell the roses of Scripture. Ask the Lord to lead you into an intimate knowledge of His Word. Meditate slowly on the words and think deeply about what is written. Stay with it daily, and over time you will quiet the noises inside and outside and begin to hear the Voice of God afresh. And when that Voice comes, so comes the power. Your eyes will be opened, and your understanding quickened, and chains will fall away. New hope and fresh possibilities await us as we come into this intimacy with Him. All are invited, all are welcome!

The Common Fault of All

Mark 14:50 – And they all forsook him and fled.

As we read of the night of Jesus' betrayal, we find ourselves in a scene, depicting in graphic detail, the contrast between our Lord in perfectly calm poise and the disciples in frenzied panic and disarray. Many times, when we think of that night, we think of Judas and we wonder how he could have betrayed the Lord. We might even get a little indignant and maybe somewhat self-righteous, saying proudly to ourselves, 'I could never do that.' However, friends, it is important to realize that the potential to have the attitude of Judas lies within each of us. In fact, this verse levels the playing field and puts us all on the same ground, so to speak.

Judas was not the only traitor that night. Regardless of their insistence that they would stay with the Lord no matter what, when the pressure was on, all of the disciples forsook Him and fled. Each one made a choice to preserve his own life. Every one of them deserted Jesus at His point of deepest need. Jesus had specifically hand-picked the disciples and I believe they represent a cross-section and composite of humanity which means that we are included in the 'all' that forsook Him and fled. When we forsake someone, we abandon that person; we disregard what happens to them. When we flee, we put ourselves and the protection of our own life ahead of another's. We might even trample over others, to ensure that we reach a place of safety.

Even though it was a terrible thing that Jesus was forsaken that night, it had to be so. For the plan of God to be fulfilled, Jesus had to face complete and utter abandonment. He was abandoned, so that we might be included. He was deserted, so that we would never have to be. He was rejected, so that we could be accepted and given complete security. He endured the suffering of the cross and the spiritual torture to save us from an horrific fate that could never be fully described. He bravely faced the harsh treatment and the ruthless punishment for you and for me. Like a shield that receives the blows protecting the one behind it, He took those blows and absorbed them courageously. He was brutally afflicted; we were mercifully exempted.

In light of what we have read in this short article today, what should be our response? What is it that we are to learn? The lesson is that our inclusion and acceptance in the Father's family was not our idea. It was not based on our actions or performance, which may have been good or bad; it was God's idea. It was and still is, His will for all mankind to be blessed, happy and protected, living in His peace and security. Everything that we have from God is given as a gift and therefore it cannot be earned. It is true that we have failed, and we will, no doubt, fail again but none of that determines God's heart toward us.

Recently I watched a movie in which a man

described the fact that his adult children did not love him, but he determined that it was not their job to love him; it was his job, as a father, to love his children. God is the ultimate and perfect Father and He will never stop loving His children. So even though we may forsake Him He will never leave us nor forsake us. Thank you, Father, we accept your steadfast love. Help us to live and bask in the light of your amazing mercy and grace!

Notes:

Section Seven

<u>Comfort</u>

" *To give strength and hope; to ease the grief or trouble of another.*

Merriam-Webster

The God of all Comfort

2 Corinthians 1:3 – Blessed be God, even the Father of our Lord Jesus Christ, the Father of mercies and the God of all comfort.

To bless God is to speak well of Him, just as to curse God would be to speak poorly. What we say about another is likely to be one of the best indicators of our relationship. If I speak well of God, then things must be well between us. We are exhorted throughout the Scripture to bless God; to exalt Him and to lift Him up. When we bless someone that means that we take the limits off them; we empower them to exceed boundaries and go way beyond the status quo. Obviously, God does not need us to take any limits off Him, but we need to have the limits taken off our view of Him. When we bless God and praise Him our hearts are enlarged, and we can receive more of who He is.

Who is this God that we are to bless? He is first and foremost, a Father. A father is one who begets life, thereby giving a future and a destiny to another. A father commences the life, but is also, committed to that life. He produces the life, and then, provides for that life. He protects, He corrects, and he directs that life. God is the Faithful Father.

Not only is He a Father, but, more specifically, he is the Father of our Lord Jesus Christ. This, of course, refers to the humanity of Jesus. As God, eternally existing, Jesus never had a beginning, but as a man, He did have a beginning and it was the Father who initiated it. When Jesus became a man by submitting to the restrictions of the womb and identifying with the natural process, He elevated our humanity; indeed, we have a noble existence and purpose. Jesus, the man, became Christ, the Lord, who brought salvation and made it available to all mankind.

God is also the Father of mercies. The world would not know mercy if it were not for Him; He initiated mercy; it had its beginnings in the Father. He gave birth to mercy and He planned the future and destiny of mercy. What would this world be like without mercy? We see some places in the world where the Word of God is banned and forbidden, and people are not given freedom to choose, and these places have become places without mercy; consequently, human life is considered worthless. Harsh and inhumane treatment is the norm and people are completely de-valued. Of course, this happens also, in our side of the world, in many hearts wherever the Word of God is rejected, and freedoms are restricted. If there is no mercy in the heart, there will be none in the life. If there is no influence of the Father, then there is a merciless life.

Mercy is what we all need, but do not always give, no doubt, we have failed as dispensers and channels of mercy. The failure itself is reason for our continued need. Just as we are not able to breathe in air for the next hour, we can only inhale and exhale the current mercy. God says that His mercy is new every morning; most likely because we need it every morning. Even the fact that God created a twenty-four-hour day is a reminder of mercy. We may have failed today, or sinned in some way, or not measured up, but just as the sun will come up over the horizon in the morning, so His mercy will be freshly prepared and waiting for us the next day. Fresh morning; fresh mercy; fresh start.

He is also called the God of all comfort. He is not the God of discouragement or despair; He is not the God of hopelessness or gloom. He is the God of all comfort; that is, He comes to us in our discouragement and despair; He is with us through it all. The word comfort itself expresses His action; it means to strengthen by being with. How striking and suggestive this word is for all of us who have opportunities daily to bring comfort to those around us.

God is the God of all comfort; He is the God of strength by presence. Just to know that He is present brings us comfort; it brings strength. He comes to us no matter what situation we might find ourselves in, or for what reason. He doesn't come to judge or condemn, He comes to comfort, He comes to bring strength by His presence. He is the God of all comfort. He has comfort for every condition or circumstance. There is no situation outside His reach.

Today, in whatever place you are; no matter your choices, or your failures, He is with you right now. Thank Him for His presence and breath in His strength and comfort.

For Every Broken Heart That Has Ever Asked Why

Matthew 27:46 – And about the ninth hour Jesus cried with a loud voice saying 'Eli, Eli lama sabachthani?' that is to say, 'My God, My God, Why have you forsaken me?'

This is one of the seven things that Jesus said while he was hanging on the cross. These few statements from Jesus have proven to be a rich heritage of blessing, strength and comfort to us. Many sermons and books have been written about them and what a powerful and enlightening study it is.

This cry of Jesus has been called the cry of anguish, or the cry of despair and it was, indeed, a haunting cry. A cry is something deeper than words; it is an expression of the heart which surpasses language. Every person on the earth knows what a heart cry is. It is a cry of instinct more than one of intellect. It is a cry of longing more than one of logic. The book of Romans tells us that all of creation is groaning; suffering under the burden of sin and suffocating from the weight of iniquity. That groan is this very cry which we are considering. Jesus, being the most spiritually sensitive man ever, was acutely aware of this period of abandonment, and he cried and groaned in total identification with forsaken mankind.

I have heard it pointed out that if you read through the Gospels carefully, you will never see Jesus address the Father as God. He always addressed him as Father, but in this dark hour of his life, He cried out to the God of the universe. Mankind is fallen and has lost his filial relationship with the Father. He cannot truly be called Father by anyone other than His children. He may be God to the entire world, but He is Father only to the family. Something mysterious was transpiring within Jesus that was so terrible, so sacred, so beyond description, that we must be very careful how we tread here. Darkness had covered the land for three hours; it may be that God mercifully hid the eyes of humanity from catching sight of things which are beyond our ability to fully understand.

Why is the basic question of the fallen race. Why me? Why is this happening to me? Why is life so difficult? Why do I keep repeating destructive patterns? Why are all these terrible things happening in the world? Why? To ask the question why is to enquire of causes; reasons that things are the way they are. We want to make sense out of our lives and circumstances. We want to find meaning and purpose in the midst of suffering. Someone has said that a man can put up with almost any 'what' as long as he has a 'why.' Jesus knew why he had to suffer; he had told his disciples ahead of time that he was going to be killed and rise again; but darkness had encircled the land; darkness had enclosed his heart; darkness had come heavily upon him, and now, darkness was coming out of him. Why, God, why?

The question of why that comes from the inside of any man always comes with his own limited perspective; he doesn't see the big picture and therefore he doesn't understand. Perspective is what one sees from their point of view; from their standpoint. I read years ago that discussing Bible truths is like climbing a mountain; if you climb up one side you see one view, but if you climb up from another side you see a different view. There are always a variety of views to look at from man's partial perspective. However, there is God's unlimited viewpoint and His infinite perspective. There was a reason that Jesus was forsaken on that day; the purpose of God was being fulfilled. He was carrying out His great plan of redemption in this sacred and horrific moment. There was a definite and meaningful why.

Fallen man is forsaken man; he is forlorn man; he is forgotten man. Why have you done this to me? Jesus is representing the whole of lost humanity which blames God for all their hardship, loss and agony. Why did you not protect me? Why are you allowing this to happen? The sense of forsakenness and abandonment is what stands between God and mankind. We sometimes have heard the phrase, 'a God-forsaken world', but maybe it is actually the Father God who is forsaken by the world. Maybe He is a 'world-forsaken God.' The Father God is truly the ultimate sufferer; he loves much, therefore he suffers much. This moment of forsakenness was equally difficult for both the Father and the Son. The Son's heart cried out in deep distress, as He represented every terrible and tragic thing that man has ever experienced as a victim and committed as a culprit. The Father's heart suffered in silent pain, as He watched His Son carry the burden and the crushing weight; the culmination of every wrong choice; the sin and the hurt of the entire world.

Tragedy, atrocity, calamity, brutality and heartbreak are the sad realities of life on earth. There is sorrow on every continent, pain in every country and grief in every home. Our deepest consolation comes to us as we understand that Jesus suffered these same things, he experienced the complete range of human emotions and he continues to suffer with us. Jesus was forsaken, deserted,

abandoned and rejected so that we could be
fully accepted and lovingly embraced; included
in the family and affirmed by the Father. No
matter what you may be facing today,
however dark and heavy your heart may be,
however many questions may be in your mind,
I pray that you would cry out to the Father
and receive His peace, His strength and His
assurance that He is walking with you through
it all. He has not forsaken you in the past and
He will never forsake you in the future. Amen!

Mercy Triumphs over Judgement

Luke 17:14 – Go show yourselves to the priests.

As Jesus was on his way to Jerusalem, ten lepers had stood at a distance down the road, and cried out for much-needed mercy. Consider the terrible circumstances that these poor men lived in; the sense of worthlessness and rejection upon being forced away from their family and friends. Perhaps the most horrific thing about being a leper was remembering a time when you were not. At one time all these men were active members of their communities. They had the love of spouses and families. They had meaningful work and the satisfaction of providing for their own. They enjoyed friends and social gatherings and they even had the hope of future good when gathering together for worship. But all of that was lost when the leprosy was discovered. They became, as the Law demanded, outcasts; they were to be separated and segregated; they were immediately torn away from all that they knew and all that they loved. The Law had spoken, and mercy stood silent in the background.

After crying out to Jesus for mercy, the first word they heard was; go. It is a strange thing that all of us hear things through our own inner filters. Sometimes even kindly spoken words are not received as such, because they come through our tainted ears into our wounded memories, and become part of our distorted conclusions. They might have felt like this was another in a long string of rejections, but we know that Jesus was indeed answering their cry with an instruction designed to urge them forward. Go. Don't stay in this place. Your leprosy has immobilized you and kept you in a hopeless and helpless state. Now, decide and choose to act, even if you do not fully understand. Don't hesitate or try and reason this out. You must do this because no one else can do it for you.

Go and show yourselves to the priests. Stand before the authority of the priests and don't hide anything; don't try to cover anything up. Be completely open, defenceless and vulnerable. This takes a tremendous amount of trust and a great deal of humility, because it is in our human nature to hide from being analysed, scrutinized and examined.

One writer has said that the self that we send out to meet God is almost always a false self. And not only with God but, also in our relationship to others, it is very easy to wear a mask and not be completely genuine. Life itself seems to teach us to be guarded and not to be open and sincere. Jesus said that we must become like children if we want to truly experience the kingdom of God. Children, in their innocence, are real; they have no preconceived, ideas or biases, and they do not understand the word; false. These ten lepers were instructed to show themselves to the priests. They were not told to build a case for why they should be treated with mercy. They were not told to describe in detail their painful history, or how they had been mistreated.

They were not told to present their credentials or their educational diplomas. No, they were told to show themselves to the priests. All we genuinely have is ourselves; our inner being; our spirit; our soul. One day we shall each stand before the Lord completely alone; without a made-up façade; without sparkling accessories; without props for support; simply our exposed self.

Jesus responded to their cry for mercy by telling them to go and show themselves to the priests. This instruction was what the Law of Moses prescribed to all who were thought to be lepers, and to all those who claimed to be cleansed of their leprosy; they were to go stand before a panel of priests. We can only imagine how this must have made them feel. What images were derived in their minds? The last time they had stood before the priests they were found to be unclean, and the sentence was harsh and final. Some of us have had to stand before one judge in a court of law, but how many of us have had to stand before a panel of judges? This would, no doubt, be extremely intimidating and they might have asked themselves why would Jesus send us to the priests? We are not healed yet. There is no change in our circumstances, however, Jesus has told us to do this.

The Law of their religion had removed them and isolated them and even made them feel non-human. That is what the Law of strict religion still does; it does not create an atmosphere of mercy. These ten men, who were labelled as outcasts, met Jesus who is Mercy manifested in the flesh. They instinctively cried out for the only answer for their desperate situation. They wanted mercy and it seemed like Jesus was giving them law, however they trusted the words of mercy; they were willing to throw themselves on the mercy of the court, so to speak. Jesus had said to go and submit to the Law; trust what Mercy has said, and the scripture tells us that as they went, they were cleansed. Mercy had spoken, it was no longer silent, and they responded in faith, trusting in the Merciful One. On that day those men received mercy and this day that we live in, is still the day of mercy. Today, no matter what we may face, we can cry out for mercy and, as always, mercy will eternally triumph over judgement! Thank God for His mercy!

Guidance through Mourning

1 Samuel 16:1 - How long will you mourn for Saul?

The world is not as it was created to be in the beginning. God's plan never included heartbreak, tragedy, loss or sorrow. Sorrow is a product of Adam's sin; it is a product of our fallen condition and the current state of things. However, even though they were never part of God's original intention for us, sorrow, loss and grief are some of the emotions that we will inevitably experience in this life, and we must know how to navigate through them, because the process of recovery is very important.

God came to Samuel and asked him how long he was going to mourn. The mourning was not wrong. God knows that we must acknowledge loss and recognize grief if we are to overcome it. We must grieve appropriately.

When we lose a loved one, we realize there must be a time of mourning. The mourning shows respect for the one you lost; it indicates the valuable place that they held in your life. They were a vital and integral part of your life and now they are gone. There needs to be a process of coming to terms with the reality that life will never be the same. Change has come and we must move forward for there is a life to be lived and a destiny to fulfill. We sometimes feel guilty about moving on in life after the loss of someone so important and so very close to us. How can we be happy and still grieve the loss?

There is a necessary thing called closure. A door unlocked is one thing, but a door left half way open doesn't seem right, especially if it's your front door. One of the basic things we were taught as a child was to close the door on the way out. An old preacher once said that there are only two things that we do in life; we enter and we leave, and how you leave one place determines how you enter another. Seasons come and seasons go, and we cannot grieve the loss of each season forever. There is a time of mourning, and then, there must be a time to accept the loss, and adjust our thinking, and renew our hope for the future. The mourning is necessary, the mourning is important, the mourning is real but, the mourning must eventually lose its paralyzing grip on us, otherwise, we will be held in the past forever.

According to our verse, the time frame of mourning is somewhat in our control. How long it lasts may be determined by our choice. How long? Should we mourn for a month? Or should we mourn for a year? Is there a fixed amount of time that someone should mourn? No! Everyone is different and every situation and circumstance is also different. There are no formulas for mourning. Mourning is not mechanical; it is biological. It is organic, it is alive, and it is a very personal process. We must walk through it step by step, trusting God to lead us into a place of healing and restored hope. We will know when the time is right.

We should also realize that loss is

experienced in many different ways. We do not always have to lose a loved one to experience loss. There are many other forms of loss which should also be grieved appropriately. There is the loss of employment, which issues in many other challenges. There is the loss of friendship. There is the loss of innocence. There is the loss of a sense of destiny. Likewise, we can lose the ability to dream. We can lose the ability to laugh. We can, and do, lose all kinds of things in life and we must acknowledge the loss, mourn accordingly, and then, move on. If we do not recognize loss, we will never recognize the new things put in front of us. New opportunities await all of us, but if we are stuck in the debilitating and overwhelming effects of sorrow, we will not be able to see them when they come.

When we know that what we have lost was originally given by God it becomes harder to leave it in the past and go forward into our future. Saul was the man chosen by God but because of his choice he forfeited the honour of continuing as king. Many times, we have difficulty with letting go of something that was initiated by God and was such a blessing to us. However, there are always going to be transitions; change inevitably comes; nothing in this life lasts forever. We intuitively know this, but it is not easy to live out. A wonderful lady said to me once, when we were going through a very difficult season, that a big part of the role of a pastor, or spiritual leader, is to help people say hello and to say goodbye. That statement rings true to me. Just think of our lives; we say hello to elementary school and we say goodbye to it; we say hello to a job, or career, and we say goodbye to it; we say hello to our thirties and we say goodbye to them; we say hello to people we love and we say goodbye to them. That actually sums up our lives; we say hello to the world in birth and we say goodbye in death, and in between there are many hellos and goodbyes.

Life is a series of transactions and transitions; entrances and exits; beginnings and endings; saying hello and saying goodbye. Like a trapeze artist, there is a time to hang on and a time to let go, and the timing for each is all-important. Be encouraged, friend, you may feel alone and even lost, but you are not. Take your time, we cannot force the process. Choose your counsellors wisely and let your Heavenly Father wrap His arms around you. Let all the heaviness go and rest in His everlasting arms. He will guide through this season of life and His powerful grace will prevail in you. Amen!

The Whispering God

1 Kings 19:11, 12 - And, behold, the LORD passed by, and a great and strong wind tore the mountains, and broke in pieces the rocks before the LORD; but the LORD was not in the wind: and after the wind an earthquake; but the LORD was not in the earthquake: And after the earthquake a fire; but the LORD was not in the fire: and after the fire, a still small voice.

The still, small voice that we read about here was like a gentle breeze, it was soft words, in fact, it was a quiet, whispering voice. Let's consider this thought today; the Almighty, All-Powerful God is also the Whispering God.

A whisper implies relationship and intimacy. Lovers whisper. Close friends may whisper. A confidante may whisper secrets. A little girl and her mother might snuggle and whisper. For a whisper to be effective, the one who whispers must be in close proximity. The one who is whispered to must also be close by; near enough to hear the soft breath.

To hear the soft whisper, we must be able to tune out the noise and the clamour of this world. Remember that it is a still, small voice, so only those who slow down, and become still and lower themselves, will hear. We must clear out the other voices and external distractions.

However, the voices on the inside may be louder and more difficult to silence than the voices on the outside. The voices within may be the voice of failure and regret, the voice of anxiety and fear, the voice of sorrow and pain, the voice of grief and loss, or the voice of despair and depression.

A whisper is more closely related to the breath than it is to the vocal chords. A whisper from God carries within it His very breath. He breathed life into Adam, in the beginning, and He breathes life into us through the whisper.

It a custom designed whisper. It is specifically crafted and intended to answer our every need. A whisper invites imagination. It is designed to stir the heart and excite the spirit to dream again. You can do it. You have what it takes. You are loved. You are capable. You are gifted. You have a purpose.

Our Father is the Great I Am. He is everything that we could ever possibly need. He is the whispering I Am. Listen, and you will hear Him whisper to you. I am your Healer. I am your Physician. I am your caregiver. I am your strength. I am your nurse. I am your specialist. I am your treatment. I am your diagnosis and your prognosis. I have taken care of this already. I am breathing life and strength into you now. Every cell of your body is receiving the life of God. Every fibre of your being is pulsating with divine life. Do not fear. I am with you. I am here on your behalf. I will never leave you nor forsake you.

He whispers peace to the troubled heart. He whispers strength to the ones who are fainting. He whispers His faith to the ones who may be questioning theirs. He is the whispering God; he is never taken by surprise. He is never caught off guard; He has foreseen every difficulty. He has planned for every contingency. When the heaviness of life comes, and the weight of burdens unimaginable seems to be pressing the very life out of you, He whispers His strength. He whispers His power. He whispers grace and forgiveness, a fresh start, and mercy, which is new every morning. He whispers wisdom and guidance; solutions to problems and answers to questions.

As you whisper back to God, it is a whisper of gratitude. Thankful for who He is. Thankful for who you are. Thankful for what you have. Thankful for the experiences of life; the sights, the sounds, the emotions, the feelings, the people, the trust, even the betrayals and the losses; you are just simply grateful to be alive and to know God and to know others. I have loved, and I have been loved. I have hurt, and I have been hurt. I have forgiven, and I have been forgiven. I have trusted, and I have been trusted. I have kissed, and I have been kissed.

I have lived, I have loved, I have gained, I have lost and, through it all, I have grown, I have become more aware, I see, I hear, I touch, I smell, I taste; I am human.

Thank you, Father, for these whispers from your heart; you are, indeed, the Whispering God.

Twelve Years of Joy and Twelve Years of Sorrow

Luke 8:42, 43 - For he had one only daughter, about twelve years of age...And a woman having an issue of blood twelve years...

Here we have an interesting comparison of a season of time in two lives; Jairus' daughter and the woman with the issue of blood.

The young girl is the only child of Jairus and his wife, and we can just imagine how much joy she brought to them. It is possible that they had tried for more than one child, however, their daughter was all they were given and so she became the only precious little one; the bright light bringing great meaning to their lives. Anyone who has had the privilege of having children born into their family knows that life is never the same again. Life takes on a new focus and all of it is centered on the care, nurture and protection of that sweet little one. Even hard-hearted men are quickly softened by the arrival of a baby, and especially so when that baby is a girl.

Twelve years of having a beautiful little girl in the house. Twelve years of joy and laughter. Twelve years of snuggles and giggles and playing house. Twelve years of innocent curiosity about the world. The first words, the first steps, the first day of school; all such joy-filled moments fixed in the memory and cherished by parents.

Twelve wonderful years were spent watching this beautiful girl grow into a young woman. Jairus may have thought of the day when a young man would come knocking on the door looking for his daughter. Our little treasure. How will we ever let her go? Raising children is a bittersweet experience because at some point, you realize that they will not remain in this place of young innocence for long.

Every life is like a river that constantly

moves never stops. The water is never the same each moment; truly we never step into the same river twice. The water has gone by us unable to be contained in our hands. The lives of our children are like the river; they also flow by us and we cannot hold on to them; we cannot keep them at a certain age. Oh, how we would love to keep our little ones in the place of innocence where the world can never hurt them, but alas, it cannot be so. To live is to love and to love is to give away and give away we must, or we will hinder our children and limit their future. The truth is these little ones are not ours; they are the children of God; they belong to Him; we are simply stewarding.

Jairus and his wife had enjoyed those years and they seemed to have gone by so quickly, but for a certain lady who lived in the same region, the last twelve years were not enjoyed and did not go by quickly; they were a long, drawn-out and dark nightmare.

Twelve years this dear woman had this condition and no matter how she sought relief, it never improved, it only got worse. Twelve years of struggling to keep her hopes up that, one day, life could go back to normal. Twelve years of physicians, poking and prodding and asking questions. Twelve years of various treatments, some of which, may have bordered on torture. Twelve years of suffering the loss of friendships and simple pleasures.

Up until the time when her affliction came, she was most probably a wife and a mother and had enjoyed the blessing of family life. We know that she was a woman who had a measure of wealth and, no doubt enjoyed the social status that comes with having means. The community events and fundraisers, the family gatherings and celebrations had all become a faint memory.

The loss of blood ran parallel to the loss of everything else in her life; her blood ebbed slowly away; her dreams ebbed slowly away; her strength receded little by little; her faith receded little by little. As she grew weaker, it seemed her misgivings grew stronger. Why has this happened to me? Have I done something wrong? Has God forsaken me?

The strict and harsh religious people loved to look down their noses and point fingers at the suffering ones. She endured twelve years of accusation and judgement; misunderstanding and mishandling; criticism and condemnation. Twelve long years.

What season of life are we in? Is it a season of joy, or a season of sorrow? For undeniably, life brings both, and Jesus is present in both. As a friend, He laughs with us in our joys and records them so we can remember, and as a comforter, He cries with us in our sorrows, and removes the pain from our memory. He is the Great Companion and Consoler who never abandons or forsakes us. Twelve years of joy, twelve years of sorrow.

God; the Generous Giver

*Psalm 84:11 – For the Lord God is a sun
and shield: the Lord will give grace and
glory: no good thing will he withhold from
them that walk uprightly.*

We have all heard the old saying, 'A picture
is worth a thousand words,' and it is, of
course, very true. However, if it were not for
words there would be no way to describe the
picture that you were seeing. Words paint
pictures, and God's Word paints pictures that
only He, the Master Artist, could paint. In the
verse above we are being given a vivid word-
picture; the Lord God is a sun and a shield.

The sun is an ever-radiating, never-
diminishing, constantly shining, sphere of
light. It is the very definition of faithfulness,
which means it is entirely trustworthy and
absolutely reliable and it will always be there.
The sun never changes; it is predictable. We

know exactly what it is going to do, and so, we can plan our lives accordingly. The Lord God is like the sun; He is steady and faithful and therefore, in one sense, He is predictable. We know what He is going to do because we know what He has said in His Word and so we can plan our lives accordingly. The sun is not erratic; it is not fickle, and it does not act in a random fashion. Of course, I am not saying that we know every method by which God will do certain things, or the time frame within which He will do it; I am simply saying that by knowing his Word we can know His will and, therefore, we can have a measure of security and confidence in what He desires for us.

The sun is our planet's source of life; it is always generously lavish with its life-bringing rays. Our Father is, likewise, very generous; Jesus said that He makes His sun to rise on the evil and the good; He is no respecter of persons; He values all people. What He will do for one, He will do for all. Any parent knows that if you have more than one child you cannot, or at least, should not, show favouritism; what you do for one child you will do for all. Good parents love all their children equally and desire only the very best for them. The children, however, by their attitude, determine how they are dealt with by the parents. If your child is defiant and displaying a very bad attitude, then you may have to respond by dealing stronger than you would like to. Conversely, if your child has misbehaved and then accepts responsibility and is very sorry, then you, no doubt, will respond in a much more lenient fashion. Likewise, we also, can determine the response of God toward us.

The sun's rays, while bringing much needed heat and life, can also be very harmful. We must be careful not to gaze directly into the sun; our eyes can be damaged by the brilliance of its light. Likewise, our skin must be covered and protected or it, too, could be damaged by the sun's penetrating rays. There must be a deep respect for the power of the sun; not a fear, but a wise reverence. Experienced electricians teach their apprentices that the first thing to learn is that this power is far greater than humans and it better be respected; one must not dare to have a cavalier or flippant attitude toward that power.

Not only is the Lord God a sun but, He is also a shield. When we hear the word shield, we usually think of armour and warfare. The shield is that which stands between the weapon and the person against whom the weapon is aimed. The shield takes the blow for us, it absorbs the impact and protects us from harm. The thought of God being our shield gives us a lot of confidence to go out and face life bravely; as we walk closely with God, whatever comes our way must pass through the shield first.

The shield represents the fatherly, protective aspect of God's heart. He is a watchful and observant Father who guards the wellbeing of His children. Like any good parent, He wants no harm to come to the child; He issues warnings of impending danger; He teaches the child to wisely obey laws of safety and He provides an environment of security.

Our God is both the sun and the sunscreen; He is the power source and the protection from that power; He is the burning fire and the containing fireplace; He gives both grace and glory.

Grace is God's ability to change any situation. He can make anything out of anybody. It does not matter where you or I may have been, or how sinful we may have been, because there is no circumstance that can keep His grace from turning it into something good. Grace empowers us to release the hurt, forget the past and walk forward in the plan of God.

Glory is that aspect of God that defies definition, it transcends our finite minds because it contains the fulness of God and His many attributes. One Hebrew scholar has said that the glory of God is every conceivable or possible good; it goes beyond our capacity to fully understand. The glory of God contains within it everything that we could ever need or desire; it represents ultimate fulfilment.

Be encouraged, friends, there is within our

Father God a deep longing to give. It is His nature to give; He is not withholding from us. In fact, He is so good that we could never fully describe His goodness. All we must do is open our heart and bask in the sunlight of His grace and glory.

The God Who Wipes Away all Tears

Revelation 21:4 - And God shall wipe away all tears from their eyes; and there shall be no more death, neither sorrow, nor crying, neither shall there be any more pain: for the former things are passed away.

We are invited to preview a day that is coming in which everything will be perfectly new, being restored to God's original plan. At that time one of the first things God will do is to wipe away all tears from our eyes. What a statement of His heart; He is indeed the ultimate Father. How intimate and tender; how personal and affectionate; that the Almighty God is attracted to the cry of His child; His heart yearns to bring comfort. When our young ones hurt themselves, or are upset about something, we hold them close and gently wipe their tears from their face. We whisper comforting things to them to fill their hearts with peace. We want our children to be reassured; we never wish upon them a sense of fear or uncertainty. We received all of these good qualities, as parents, from the example and the nature of our Heavenly Father. He was, at the beginning, He is now, and He always will be, the true essence of Fatherhood; protection, provision, security and peace.

The answer to our question of whether there will be tears in Heaven is settled here; there will indeed be tears. Tears might be shed for several different reasons; we know that there are tears of joy and gratitude, as well as tears of remorse and sorrow. Some tears come from the loss of someone special, and some come just as an emotional release from pressure. The tears mentioned in our verse seem to suggest that they are connected to the memory of death, sorrow, crying and pain. As we look back from Heaven's perspective, we will see the whole of life and how things interacted; we may see the missed opportunities, the neglect of priorities and the regret of poor choices, and tears will fall. Thankfully, though, that will be the end of our tears; they will be wiped away forever.

The highest desire and will of God for His family has always been the same, and we can see it plainly stated in this verse. No more death. No more sorrow. No more crying. No more pain. That is the will of God. However, we live in this fallen and imperfect world where these things are a present reality and must be dealt with accordingly, and thank God, we have been equipped to deal with them; we are not left powerless.

Imagine a world where there was no death; where everything that was alive remained alive forever. We can hardly imagine it because we have only known death; in fact, all of humanity's history is a story of death. They were born; they lived; they died. Death came into the world because of what we call the fall of man. When Adam chose to disobey the instructions of God, he chose death; he chose to place distance between himself and God and take on a new, self-centered nature.

Death is not necessarily the end of life; it is separation from life. When the rose is cut from the bush it is separated from its life source; the law of death has been set in motion and it will eventually overtake it. Spiritual death likewise is a separation, not cessation; the spirit of man has been separated from God our life source, just as Paul wrote to the Ephesians, 'We were separated from the life of God.' Physical death is a separation of the body from the spirit and one day each of us will succumb to the unavoidable moment of our last breath.

Sorrow is connected to loss and this life inevitably brings much loss in many ways. There is the loss of the innocence we once knew; there is the loss of dignity and self-worth; perhaps a loss of trust; loss of integrity; or, the loss of employment. Many of us have also experienced the loss of health; loss of relationship and the ultimate loss of a loved-one. Jesus came to seek and to save that which is lost, and all the sorrow and loss associated with it.

The cry of mankind is one of instinct, not necessarily, intellect; we intuitively know that things are not as they should be. When we see the pictures of children suffering poverty and hunger, we know that could never be God's plan for them. When we hear of disasters and calamities resulting in the loss of human life we know that God could never be the cause of it. The Book of Romans refers to the groaning that is resident throughout creation. The groan does not need to be articulated because it is a universally felt cry of the heart.

Physical pain serves as an alarm that something is wrong in our body and that is a good thing, but, emotional and psychological pain that results from the abuse or, mistreatment from another human being, is a terrible thing. Unfortunately, there is no one who hasn't felt the sting of heartbreak and agony which, in this current life, is inevitable.

This precious verse is a word from God that fills our heart with hope. The good news is that one day everything will be okay. All wrongs will be made right. All relationships will be fully restored. All hurts will be healed. One day all these dreadful things will be a thing of the past and only a faint memory. They belong to a class of things called the former things and they will all pass away and come to an end. So why not get used to the idea of a God who wipes away the tears of His children? You are invited to come and snuggle up close in the arms of your Father and let Him be to you what he longs to be; the God who wipes away every tear; the Father of mercies and the God of all comfort.

The Weeping Christ

John 11:35 – Jesus wept.

Jesus is the perfect picture of a man created in the image of God and He is the only man who has never lost his God-given identity and purpose. He represents all that the Father God originally intended for us. He came to live a life before us and exemplify the heart of the Father God. As this man-of-all-men stood before the grave of His dear friend, Lazarus, He wept.

Jesus wept because death was never part of the plan of God; it was, and still is, an enemy, a bully and an intruder into the life of mankind. Death and all that is associated with it is foreign to God, it is not in His heart or His plan. God is light and in Him there is no darkness, and He is also life and in Him there is no death.

Jesus wept because of His friend. He wept

because of Mary and Martha. He wept because the loss of a loved one and the heavy sorrow that comes with it was never His heart for us. Just as any good parent does not want their child to suffer sorrow and heartache, so Jesus felt the loss of Lazarus and his family, and He felt the collective loss of all humanity.

Jesus wept for Lazarus because he had been taken much too soon. He wept because the religious culture had taught them that God was the one who had taken him. Our gracious Father has been lied about, He has been misrepresented and slandered throughout the centuries. He does not take; He is the supreme giver. He does not need to kill people so that He can have them in Heaven with Him; wouldn't that be considered extremely selfish? Let it be said with great emphasis and constant repetition; He is not the taker. He does not take; however, He does receive those that leave. God is not the author of death!

Jesus wept because of humanity's loss of faith; they could not believe in the power of

His resurrection life. They could not see beyond what their senses were telling them. They could not see how God could answer this situation. They could not see past the horizon of their own knowledge; they were imprisoned in their hopelessness and because of who He is, our compassionate Christ shed tears for them.

Jesus wept because man had lost his identity and his purpose for living. The people of Earth have been lied to, and the lie has brought untold misunderstanding, it has distorted our once-clear vision. Confusion and despair, indeed, the death of hope has brought us to the brink of self-destruction.

Jesus wept because He wasn't afraid to weep; He wasn't ashamed of His emotions and deep feelings. He wept because He felt the sting of God's plan gone awry. He wept because He came to bear the burden of all men; He identified so keenly with the universal human struggle. He wept because things were not as they should be, and He longed to put things right. He wept because He was, and still is, the Intercessor who pleads with God for lost and downtrodden souls.

Jesus is the ultimate Man and so all who follow Him will also follow Him in His weeping over all of mankind. His weeping was a prayer and His tears were a plea; it was a way of drawing close to the sufferer and it was a wordless appeal to the Father's heart. We, in a Christlike spirit, must follow Him in this tearful compassion for others.

Oh, that the heart of Jesus would manifest through us in weeping, groaning, pleading and claiming. Weeping for the wayward ones, groaning over the destruction of precious lives, pleading the merits of the sacrifice of Christ and claiming the fulfilment of the promises of God.

Jesus wept and the Father heard. Jesus wept and the Father responded. Jesus wept and the Spirit moved. Jesus wept and Martha hoped. Jesus wept and Mary trusted. Jesus wept and Lazarus rose. Jesus wept!

About the Author

Doug's deepest desire is to see the fulfillment of what the prophet Isaiah spoke, that the 'Earth would be full of the knowledge of God, as the waters cover the sea'. In order to fulfill this God-given desire, he has, over the years, served in a variety of roles in the local church; Home Group Leader, Men's Group Leader, Church Elder, Assistant Pastor, Senior Pastor, and more recently as a prolific and passionate writer. Doug lives in Kelowna, B. C., Canada with his beautiful wife, Sue. Married for thirty-seven years, they have three grown sons and one precious granddaughter, Willa.

:

Connect With
Douglas J Glada

A Minute in the Word

http://dougglada62.blogspot.com/

On Facebook:

https://www.facebook.com/dglada62

First Page Solutions:

https://firstpagesolutions.ca/publisher/author/
douglas-j-glada

Made in the USA
Middletown, DE
05 December 2019